Ahead of Change

Constantin Malik is an expert in management cybernetics. He holds a Master Degree in Law and earned a Doctoral Degree in Psychology having integrated crowd psychology, managerial cybernetics and law to new approach on government. He is the secretary of the board of directors at Malik Management, an international knowledge organization in the field of general management consulting and education. He lives in St. Gallen, Switzerland.

Constantin Malik

Ahead of Change

How Crowd Psychology and Cybernetics Transform the Way We Govern

Campus Verlag
Frankfurt/New York

Bibliografische Information der Deutschen Nationalbibliothek:
Die Deutsche Nationalbibliothek verzeichnet diese Publikation in der Deutschen Nationalbibliografie. Detaillierte bibliografische Daten sind im Internet unter http://dnb.d-nb.de abrufbar.
ISBN 978-3-593-39204-2

Umschlaggestaltung: Guido Klütsch, Köln
Satz: Fotosatz L. Huhn, Linsengericht
Druck und Bindung: Beltz Druckpartner, Hemsbach
Gedruckt auf Papier aus zertifizierten Rohstoffen (FSC/PEFC).
Printed in Germany

Besuchen Sie uns im Internet: www.campus.de

To my parents

Contents

German preface for editionMALIK

Die alte Welt vergeht,
weil eine neue Welt entsteht.

Wirtschaft und Gesellschaft gehen durch eine der tiefgreifendsten Umwandlungen, die es geschichtlich je gab. Als Begriff wählte ich 1997 dafür »Die Große Transformation«, denn bereits damals war das Ausmaß des heraufziehenden epochalen Wandels deutlich zu sehen. Was heute lediglich als eine finanzielle und ökonomische Krise zu eng gesehen wird, kann weit besser als die Geburtswehen der neuen Welt des 21. Jahrhunderts verstanden werden.

In dieser neuen Welt werden Organisationen eine höhere Ebene des Funktionerens erreichen. Sie werden doppelt so gut wie bisher funktionieren, aber nur die Hälfte des Geldes dafür benötigen. Die universelle Herausforderung wird für sie das Meistern von bisher noch nie erfahrener Komplexität durch neues Management sein.

Geld ist dafür aber weit weniger wichtig als Intelligenz, Vorstellungskraft, Information, Kommunikation und Gestaltungswille. Das neue Wissen hierfür und darauf gestützt neue, biokybernetische Lösungen sind bereits da. Deren Kern sind die ®Evolutionären Naturgesetze aus Kybernetik und Bionik für das Selbstorganisieren und Selbstregulieren. Diese Gesetze zu verstehen und sie zu nutzen, ist das neue Kapital der neuen Welt und die Grundlage für Leadership von Personen und Organisationen.

Die editionMalik ist die Plattform für das zuverlässige Funktionieren von Organisationen in der hochkomplexen Umwelt des 21. Jahrhunderts. Sie ist die systemische Orientierungs- und Navigationshilfe für Leader, die den Wandel vorausdenken und -lenken.

Fredmund Malik
St. Gallen, Januar 2010

Über Malik sagt der Doyen des Managements, Peter F. Drucker:

»Fredmund Malik has become the leading analyst of, and expert on, Management in Europe as it has emerged in the last thirty years – and a powerful force in shaping it ... He is a commanding figure – in theory as well as in the practice of Management.«

Author's preface

Wars, revolutions and financial manias are not a necessity. There are ways to prevent them. There are ways to transform the way we govern to ensure a functioning society. What it takes is to be ahead of change is to anticipate change and prepare for it. For this, new methods and instruments are needed – and a whole new way of thinking. Crowd Psychology and Management Cybernetics lead the way.

We have the unique chance today to change something that appears to be an everlasting law: that mankind needs a complete breakdown before it can achieve further progress. We have this chance because today we have the tools to change it.

The crisis we are witnessing is, in my opinion, far from over. And it has the capacity to become the worst crisis this world has seen in centuries. But it is not too late to prevent a disaster. The methods pursued until now, however, lead straight to it. This book offers an alternative way.

What I present here to the reader is a revised version of my dissertation, which I finished in 2006. Looking back at the last two years, it becomes clear to me that I should have made it available sooner. Although four years seems like a long time, and one would think that a lot may have changed since, I am even more convinced today that the direction I pursued was, and still is, right and that the suggestions in my book remain valid and have even gained in urgency.

I want to thank my father, Prof. Dr. Fredmund Malik, who has always been my greatest source of knowledge, inspiration and support and from whom I have learned everything. Further thanks go to Prof. Dr. Linda Pelzmann for encouraging me and allowing me to think and go beyond academic frontiers; Robert R. Prechter jun. and Matt Lampert of Elliott Wave International and the Socionomic Institute for their input and support.

Constantin Malik
Davos, January 2010

Part I – Delay

1. Law and Future

1.1 Law's delay

Law lags behind society. Ever since legal systems have existed – probably ever since consciously set rules were laid down – the law has trailed societal developments. It is something that is immanent in our legal and political systems. First, there needs to be a change of some sort. Then we go and try to regulate the new and integrate it properly into our presently given structure. It does not look like there has ever been a time when legal rules were actually ahead of changes in society.

Of course there has always been the attempt to directly shape society and its future. Monarchs and dictators did so. Their will was the law. But this is a completely different matter because they did not anticipate future developments. They did not try to see what the future might bring so they could pass laws applicable to these future cases. They tried to create the future themselves. To some extent this might even have worked, but true societal change has found them unprepared time and again. Revolutions and wars prove this. Changes in society are stronger than monarchs or parliaments. They have the power to sweep away existing structures and institutions. And it appears there has never been a time when such changes were anticipated and regulated – and thereby mitigated – in advance.

Today, as society seems to move at an ever-increasing speed and all spheres of life are getting increasingly complex and complicated, the time lag between change and regulation seems to grow as well, since our lawmaking bodies are not able to keep up with the pace set by society. It takes a long time for a law to be passed. Experts need to be consulted, problems need to be cleared up and agreements need to be reached before a bill can be passed. At the same time, governments take on more and more matters that they consider to be in need of regulation. Meanwhile, society moves on.

Most scholars do not seem to mind. In fact, they seem to consider it normal that society is ahead of the law. John Morison of the School of Law at

Queen's University Belfast writes that »Legislation must always follow along behind changes in public opinion. There is thus, inevitably, a lag between law and real life ...«[1] According to Georg Müller lawmaking »... often is less a matter of shaping future developments and more a process of adapting the law to preceding changes in the value judgments of society.«[2] And another scholar writes: »The law always follows progress. Technology, the economy, and science are constantly creating new necessities for regulation required of the lawmaking process.«[3]

1.2 A future unknown

So the problem is well known, yet it does not appear to be considered a problem. Or it is recognised as a problem, but is hampered by the age-old mantra of »Why bother if we cannot change it anyway?« I actually do believe that this is the very reason why the time lag between changes in society and legal regulation is not addressed more often: Most scholars think that we cannot change it. And when you think about it: How could it be otherwise? It is all a matter of knowing the future – and we do not know the future. We have no means of peeking into the future and forecasting or anticipating future events and developments (or so we believe), which in turn would allow us to make adjustments ahead of time. The only thing that we know about the future is that it is uncertain. So surprises, be they good or bad, cannot be helped. We are doomed to sit and wait what might happen and then try to make the best out of it.

It is of course not entirely true that everybody thinks in this manner. Especially where the economy is concerned we are confronted with forecasts every day: There are experts who predict the state of the economy next year; they predict recessions and inflations; there are stock market analysts who tell us which way the markets are going to develop next month, if Microsoft's stocks are going to rise and if oil prices will come down. They try to guess and anticipate what the future might bring and they do so with a lot of confidence.

In the legal field there is less talk of predicting the future especially when it comes to legislative action. Of course, one can argue that legislation is always for the future because laws may not – with few exceptions – be applied retrospectively and they are passed to regulate present and future cases. However, such future cases are never genuinely new but are of the same nature as the current problems and questions for which the law has been made. Consequently, laws do not genuinely anticipate new future developments and regulate them in advance. They are made for today and are »merely« applicable to future issues of the same kind.

Scanning the research on this subject and looking at how scholars are dealing with »law and future« as a pair, three different fields of interest can be distinguished:

1.2.1 Methodology

The first field of interest looks at the methods of both lawmaking and the application of law and how it might change in the future. How is legal interpretation going to develop? What kind of impact could and should new approaches such as the »Economic Analysis of Law« have on jurisdiction?[4] How will the competition between different legal systems, e.g. in the European Union, affect legislation?[5] Currently, it is especially the increasing internationalization and the growing convergence of European continental code law and Anglo-Saxon case and common law that are of major interest here.[6]

1.2.2 Shaping

The second field looks at the possibilities that we have to influence the future directly by means of law. If the future is uncertain and it is not possible to regulate developments in advance since we cannot foresee them, then the question arises what means of law we have to create the future ourselves and steer society in the desired direction.[7]

1.2.3 »Futurology«

There are scholars who try to anticipate the future under legal aspects. Their concern is to foresee what the future might look like, what challenges there are going to be with which society will have to cope and how the law could help to meet these challenges.[8] This will be the subject matter of this book. Our main focus will not be to see how we could design the future by means of law so that it suits our wishes (it looks as if this were possible only to quite a limited extent anyway[9]). We will, quite on the contrary, merely look at how it might be possible to »cushion« what will come by anticipating it. Our concern will be to see whether it is not possible to regulate future developments prior to their occurrence – and not after they have hit. For this, however, the »futurology« that is being conducted today is useless. What is considered futurology today can never lead to genuine anticipation of future events and developments.

On closer inspection, we find that the way with which those scholars concerned with future issues try to tackle the problem will never help us close the time gap between law and society. The reason is that their approach is linear extrapolation. They extrapolate present trends into the future as a means of forecasting. They look at statistical data of demographic facts and try to guess what this might mean for the situation in fifty years' time; they look at the problems we have with new technologies or with fundamentalism or other phenomena of our time, and on this basis, imagine certain scenarios for the future for which they then recommend appropriate action. With regard to the economy, Robert J. Shiller of Yale University writes: »Lacking an established theory of the ultimate causes of economic fluctuations, forecasters tend to rely on simple extrapolation of trends or on assumptions that past patterns will repeat themselves.«[10]

Such an approach will no doubt lead to some helpful insights but it will not lead to genuine anticipation. This holds true for all fields, be it the legal sciences, the economy, politics or sociology. Linear extrapolation cannot help anticipate the future. The reason why not is that trends change. True and valuable forecasting has to deal with the question of why and when trends change and what this implies. If trends did not change we would not even need forecasting. It would simply be a question of logical deduction. If the weather were always fine, nobody would be interested in the weather forecast. The trend of the past few days would tell us what the weather would be like tomorrow. But, as we all know, the weather does change and the weather forecast is there to tell us when it will change and whether the future trend means rain or droughts or hurricanes.

Robert Prechter, jun., of whom we shall hear much more later on, says:

»Trend extrapolation is the crudest form of technical analysis, and it is employed by nearly all conventional analysts, though they rarely realize it. Mainstream social and economic forecasting has forever been a practice of extrapolating present and recent conditions and trends into the future. More specifically, apparent predictions are simply (1) descriptions of present conditions (2) multiplied by unconsciously calculated moving averages of the trends of those conditions. Obviously, in a changing world, this approach is doomed to fail. Because of this practice, both economists and futurists in general have always been notoriously optimistic at tops and pessimistic at bottoms, producing highly inaccurate forecasts of coming events.

The natural, unconscious way of anticipating reality is to observe it over time and assume that trends will continue in the same way as they have in the past. While this approach is applicable to physics, it is improper to apply it to sociology. By succumbing to the natural tendency to extrapolate, forecasters become part of each wave rather than rise above it.«[11]

The legal sciences illustrate this quite well. In the years before and around the turn of the new millennium, and to this day, a lot has been written about the challenges the law is about to face in the 21st century.[12] However, all the challenges that scholars mention are products of problems that we already have – or at least we have already created the conditions for them, so it is simply a matter of time for them to occur. Biotechnology and genetics, religious fundamentalism, globalization, environmental issues, overpopulation – these problems are with us already, or at least certain to be upon us in a matter of time, because of the present situation. This extrapolation of trends, however, is no solution to the problem at all.

In connection with trends in the financial markets the *Neue Zürcher Zeitung am Sonntag* accurately observes:

»›La hausse amène la hausse‹: High returns from shares attract more money. Investors have, however, no guarantee that the boom will continue: It is dangerous to extrapolate the future from past trends.«[13]

Sometimes a trend does not change for a long time. But it is certain to change at some point. The approach of linear extrapolation ignores this. That is why we need different means to tackle our problem. The current approach will simply ensure that when society changes direction next time our institutions will be caught by surprise once more because we have been preparing for the present instead of for the future. And the time gap between change and regulative action will be the some as usual.

1.3 The danger of delayed law

It is somewhat disturbing that there is very little talk about the fact that the law is trailing societal change and little discussion about possible means of forecasting to change this problem. After all, the fact that this situation is apparently considered to be normal by a good deal of people can have serious consequences for the stability of society and, at times, can be extremely harmful for people and assets.

If changes and developments are recognized too late – or not at all – it can, in the worst case, lead a society to the brink of collapse. Even if it is recognized that some developments may have undesired or even devastating consequences, it might, after a certain point, already be too late for corrective measures. When a revolt or revolution breaks out, it is normally too late

MAJOR LAWS CREATED TO PROTECT INVESTORS		
Act	**Purpose**	**Preceded By**
1933 and 1934 Banking Act and Securities Exchange Act	Separates commercial and investment banking, creates SEC as market regulators	Stock market crash of 1929 and ensuing bear market removes nearly 90% of Dow value
1940 Investment Company Act and Investment Advisors Act	Regulates investment companies and advisors	Market decline of 25% from October 1939 to May 1940
1970 Securities Investor Protection Act	Creates Securities Investor Protection Corporation and insurance from broker defaults	Market decline of 30% from April 1969 to June 1970
1974 Employee Retirement Income Security Act	Regulates pension funds	Long bear market from December 1972 to September 1974 takes the Dow down 40%
1988 Insider Trading and Securities Fraud Enforcement Act	Increases penalties and liabilities for insider trading and fraudulent activities	Stock market crash of 1987 takes Dow down over 40%
2002 Public Company Accounting Reform and Investor Protection Act	Increases regulation of auditors, lengthens punishment for white collar crimes, and creates more corporate fraud laws	2 ½ year bear market reduced Dow by 35%, Nasdaq declines 75%

Figure 1: Laws for Investor Protection in the 20th Century

Source: Nofsinger, John/Kenneth, Kim: Protecting Investors (not), 2003, as republished in Prechter, Robert R.: Pioneering Studies in Socionomics (2003)

to prevent violence and bloodshed. When a stock market mania is in full progress, it is probably too late to prevent a crash. Preventative measures should have been taken prior to it, but this is only possible if the course of a development is recognized in time.

It is also possible that, due to an inability to foresee the course of a social development or due to a misjudgment of it, laws are passed which actually boost this development and thereby worsen things instead of »cushioning« them. A perfect example of this is a study of investor protection legislation in the United States in the 20th century conducted by John Nofsinger and Kenneth Kim, both professors at Washington State University.[14] They found out that legislative action in this sector actually follows investor sentiment. It seems that representatives in Congress are subject to the same attitude as ordinary people, thereby passing laws which are in accordance with society's overall sentiment. Figure 1 gives an overview of major laws passed in the 20th century to protect investors together with the law's purpose and the reason why it was passed in terms of the event that triggered legislative action. Note that these laws meant to protect investors were passed after a stock market decline or a crash. Investors would have needed protection before that. The timing is actually counterproductive.

Figure 2 gives an overview of laws passed to loosen investor protection and thereby to make investing easier for people. Note that, again, these laws were passed at exactly the wrong time, namely after a substantial stock market rise. Stock markets were steering towards a crash and it was then that investors would actually have needed protection. Instead, loosening restrictions meant fueling the mania.

It is not difficult to tell that it should have been the other way around. People need protection when they are too enthusiastic and likely to act irrationally and hastily. On the other hand, they do not need protection after a crash or a stock market decline. It is then that investing should be made easier to support the markets and the economy.

The example shows that legislative action in this field tends to make things worse as it supports the overall trend:

»Our point is that laws are frequently made to protect shareholders and investors. This usually occurs after people become angry over scandals and a bear market. However, these protections can also be reversed in the midst of good times. A strong economy and good bull market lead to pressure on lawmakers to loosen restrictions on corporate participants. The loosened restrictions have the potential to help push the stock market from a bull market to a bubble market. When a bubble occurs, a

REPEALS OF SOME INVESTOR PROTECTION		
Action	**Purpose**	**Preceded By**
1927 Government agency policy allowing commercial banks to issue securities	Allows commercial banks into investment banking activities	Stock market rose over 200% from 1925 to 1928
1995 Private Securities Litigation Reform Act	Limits the ability and available damages of investors suing for corporate fraud	Dow increased 60% between 1993 and 1995
1998 Securities Litigation Uniform Standards Act	Precludes plaintiffs from bringing securities actions in state courts	Dow increased 125% from 1996 to 1999
1999 Financial Services Modernization Act	Allows the combining of commercial and investment banking activities	Dow increased 125% from 1996 to 1999

Figure 2: Repeals of Investor Protection in the 20th Century

Source: Nofsinger, John/Kenneth, Kim: Protecting Investors (not), 2003, as republished in Prechter, Robert R.: Pioneering Studies in Socionomics (2003)

crash will inevitably follow. This leads to more scandals and more investor protection laws. We need to avoid this cycle.«[15]

To overcome this cycle, we need legislative action with an anticipatory character. We need lawmakers to look ahead and foresee the course of a trend so as not to be caught up in that same trend. Otherwise, trends are either not recognized at all or recognized too late or they are misjudged and action is taken that makes things worse and leads to harmful effects on society instead of contributing to its health.

1.4 Two sources of change – people and technology

It has been said that law lags behind social change. If we want to be ahead of this change, anticipate it and do something about it in advance, then we need to understand it first. We need to understand what it is, what its sources are and how it works; we need to understand its fundamental mechanisms.

If we talk about social change, then there can be two reasons why such change occurs: People and technology. Actually, there is a third reason, which could be termed *force majeure*. But, as the name implies, meteorites, earthquakes and locusts are really beyond our influencing (although man might often well be the root of a locust plague…).

The kind of change with which most people are concerned nowadays – especially regarding the question of how certain kinds of change can be regulated by means of law – is due to a change in technology. Genetics, biotechnology, the Internet and environmental questions all have to do with technological progress – or at least technological change. There is one big exception, which is globalization. New inventions and innovations no doubt change the way we live. They can revolutionize a society, destroy whole industries and create new ones. Change of this sort is clearly most relevant. But whether or not the rise of a new technology can be anticipated – and there is evidence that it can be[16] – technological change is not the subject of this book.

The kind of change that will concern us in this book is the kind of change that is brought about by human behavior. In the same way as technology changes, people change, too, in the sense that their mood changes.[17] But unlike technological change, which leads to technologies that are brand new and have never been there before, people change according to a pattern that repeats itself. When people's mood changes, they do not invent new ways of behaving. Their behavior will be the same as their ancestors' generations ago when they were in the same mood. Just how this behavior manifests itself might be different due to changed circumstances in the societal surroundings. Robert Prechter, whose theory of social mood is one of the central building blocks of this publication,[18] says that »history repeats in mood but not necessarily mode«.[19]

War, revolutions, nationalism, protectionism, racism, crime or stock market manias all have their root in a change in people's mood. And the same is true of the opposite – times of peace, liberalization, globalization, tolerance and stock market crashes. Globalization, for instance, is not something new. The world experienced international trade and the melting together of different cultures as early as the Roman Empire. Between the 10th and the 14th century we saw increasing international trade with trade routes spanning the entire European continent and connections to India, East Asia, the Middle East and Africa. There were families, such as the Fuggers, who controlled international enterprises; there were international treaties and alliances and people traveling to far-off corners of the globe.

What we are experiencing today and what so many »experts« are trying to sell us as new, as something that this world has never witnessed before, is simply a repetition of history. All that is different is the way we are globalizing. Now we have airplanes and the Internet; we have satellites and cell phones; it takes only a few hours to travel from Madrid to Mexico City or from London to Beijing instead of weeks and months. But other than that – what has changed? Again, we are dealing with the difficult integration of different cultures and customs that need to be taken into consideration when working internationally; again, we are faced with competition from abroad, and again, we are facing legal problems when it comes to transnational matters. Before, it was the harmonization of legal matters under Roman rule or the reception of the Roman Law and the Lex Mercatoria. Now, it is matters of International Private Law, multilateral treaties and organizations such as the WTO. The mode has changed – the mood repeats itself.

But there is more to phenomena such as war, revolutions, globalization or manias. They are not just caused by a change in the mood of people. They are caused by a change of mood in a large number of people – they are caused by crowds. Massive and fundamental changes in society – unless they are due to technology – involve crowds. They are the secret motor of society. This is never recognized until a war, a revolution or a mania hits; and then it is only recognized for negative events. But social change in general is largely due to crowd psychological phenomena – as we shall see[20] – and these mechanisms work beneath the surface at all times, even if we do not realize it. Indeed, as the book *The Tipping Point* very nicely shows, fads and all kinds of social trends are based on crowd behavior.[21] We just do not see it.

An understanding of social change must involve crowds. Indeed, crowds are the key to an understanding of the kind of social change that is due to human behavior. Knowledge of the individual is not enough. Only changes in large numbers of people can bring about large changes in society such as revolutions, stock market manias and globalization.

1.5 System failure

Just as we do not realize what a decisive role crowd behavior plays in the shaping of society, governments do not, either. One would think that the experts in all those think tanks all over the world clearly need to be fully aware of the mechanisms that are crucial for the development of society. Yet we can observe time and again that governments are caught by surprise by societal change – the system fails. It fail to anticipate coming changes and developments and it fails to prepare for them. The structures that today's societies have – not that this has ever been different – are neither flexible and adaptable enough nor are they stable enough to cope with changes and challenges of the scope that phenomena based on crowd psychological mechanisms can bring with them. The only exception might be Switzerland because of the tremendous role direct democracy plays. But even there, the system is far from perfect and it is better prepared only for changes that arise within its own society. But as wars and stock market manias show, changes in society can have an impact on a nation even if it occurs outside that nation.

Of course, we could say that, after all, society has survived since the breakdown of the Western Roman Empire. Indeed it has, but the question is how. A war is already a system failure. A revolution is a system failure. And although a development such as globalization does not have effects as deadly or destructive as a war or a revolution it is still a system failure if society is caught unprepared. The goal must be to keep the negative effects of any kind of change at an absolute minimum. From this perspective, our societal system has failed countless times since the end of the Roman era – and it is continuing to fail.

1.6 New perspectives

Our inability to anticipate future developments and the resulting delay of the law has been with us all along. It is, therefore, not surprising that it is accepted as normal. However, if we are to be able to prepare society for future changes and developments and make it resistant to the destructive forces which they can bring with them, we need to overcome this situation and for this we need new perspectives and new approaches. The ones that are dominant today have already failed too often and some tightening of screws at this end and some mending at that end will not save them – and therefore it will not save society. We need to find new ways of organizing our institutions – and the means that will help us do so could be **crowd psychology** and **managerial cybernetics** as I am going to suggest.

The insights that have been gained in these fields in recent years and decades are still far from being recognized, let alone implemented. This book wants to contribute to a better understanding of these two fields of science and attempt a maybe seemingly utopian but, as I hope, possible application of their findings for the sake of a reformation of our legislatures. I am convinced that if we want to see progress in our political institutions and a society that is able to protect peace and order and the freedom of the individual in the long-term it is indispensable for us to make use of the results and insights with which crowd psychology and managerial cybernetics have come up. They broaden our horizon and give us a fresh perspective on this complex system called society – and no path towards progress will lead past them.

The next two parts of this book will be dedicated to the presentation of these two fields of science: management cybernetics and crowd psychology. I will start with managerial cybernetics to demonstrate the structure that a society should have in order to be stable but also flexible and adaptable enough to cope with social changes. After that, we will have a look at crowd psychological phenomena and mechanisms with a focus on the new science of Socionomics and we will see how we can use them to anticipate future changes and developments. The last part of the book will then be dedicated to a possible application in legislation.

Part II – Stability

2. Managerial Cybernetics

The first chapter showed that the law generally trails social change in that it can sometimes take law-making bodies a considerable time to grasp and regulate the change that occurs. It should also have become clear that this can, at times, be dangerous to the overall stability of society. Social changes and developments can, as was shown in the previous chapter, be a serious threat to the freedom and peace of a society.

Although the main focus of this book is on the possibility of anticipating social developments and its use for legislation, I consider it indispensable to include a chapter on systems structure. Being able to anticipate future events would be great progress. However, unless there are structural preconditions that allow for this knowledge to be properly used and for society as a whole to adapt accordingly, this ability will be useless. If I am a pedestrian standing in the middle of the road and I can see a car approaching, then this ability to see the car is worth something only if the information is properly processed in my brain and the muscles in my legs are then told to contract so that I get off the road before the car hits me.

If I say that social changes can be threatening to the stability of society, then two things need to be clarified. First, I do not mean that we should try to prevent society from changing. This would be a harmful and impossible undertaking. Change is certain to occur. It is a necessary element of history, evolution and progress and it would be useless to try and stop it from happening. The first chapter made clear that my point is to anticipate change, not to prevent it.

Second, by stability of the system I do not mean a never-changing ever-equal condition of some sort. This would be to which the great management cybernetician Stafford Beer, to whose model the majority of this chapter is dedicated, refers as »lethal calm«.[22] If nothing ever changes in the system then there can be no adaptation to new outward or inward changes. This sort of deadlock stability would be highly undesirable. Sooner or later it would mean death.

The stability that I am referring to is, on the contrary, a state of flexibility, adaptation and alertness, and thus of constant, at least potential, change. Only the ability to change and to adapt to new developments guarantees the maximum probability of survival. W. Ross Ashby, one of the fathers of cybernetics, put it very well when he said that only a kind of stability is desirable whose »presence enables the system to combine something of flexibility and activity in performance with something of permanence».[23]

2.1 Complex systems and variety

Society is a complex system. Moreover, it is a self-organizing system, which has evolved over hundreds of thousands of years.[24] No matter how hard politicians and governments try to control every detail, most things remain unknown to them and are only known to the individual elements of the system, that is to say, to the people.[25]

The handling of complex systems requires a different method than the handling of simple systems. In a simple system there are but a few variables. They are known and can be measured more or less accurately, which allows for full knowledge of the system details and offers a chance of complete control over the system and all its details and specifics given.

Friedrich von Hayek writes that in complex systems we are necessarily restricted to the recognition of patterns because the number of variables is far too large to even know, let alone influence, them all. But, as Hayek explains, this does not mean that we are left with lesser theories because of that. Maybe such theories are not as valuable in terms of their empiric value because we are confined to »explanations of the principle«, but such is the price that we have to pay if we want to understand and deal with complex systems.[26]

So in a complex system there are far more variables than could ever be known let alone computed. In other words, much or, probably, even the overwhelming majority of what goes on within the system remains unknown. Cybernetics refers to what is going on in the system as the variety generated in the system. These two expressions need further explanation.

Cybernetics comes from the Greek word *kybernetike,* which means steersmanship, or rather *kybernetes,* steersman. Today, the word can be found in expressions such as governor, governance or government. Cybernetics can be considered the science of control or of effective organization or, as Fredmund Malik puts it, of functioning and deals with complex and dynamic systems. Again, the word control is not used in the sense of »absolute control«. It is about steering, guiding, directing: »Therefore we can understand cybernetics as steersmanship or simply the art of steering – and in more general terms the art of steering, organising and directing.«[27] Cybernetics is a transdisciplinary science (which is not identical with interdisciplinary) and looks at systems independent of their particular content:

> »It was soon discovered that there were certain principles or natural laws governing the behavior of systems under control, which regardless of the particular form or context of the system, were quite general and to which scientific expression could be given.«[28]

The time of birth of Cybernetics was the book *Cybernetics – or control and communication in the animal and the machine* by Norbert Wiener, which dates back to the year 1948. And it was actually Wiener himself who suggested the expression »Cybernetics« for this new science. The title of his book shows clearly how Cybernetics is a transdisciplinary science: It deals with the same aspects of systems no matter whether they are found in biological or artificial systems. Cybernetics is a meta-science.

Variety is the measure of complexity. It is defined as the possible number of states of a system or of »whatever it is whose complexity we want to measure«.[29] As a measure, variety is a whole number since the possible number of states can be counted. What is remarkable is that even seemingly small systems can exhibit a large potential of variety generation. As an example let us consider the following system:

Figure 3 depicts a system consisting of eight squares. If each square can either be black or white then the possible number of states is $V = 2^8 = 256$. Now if we assume that each one of the squares could in addition to black and white also be blue, then the possible number of states would be raised to

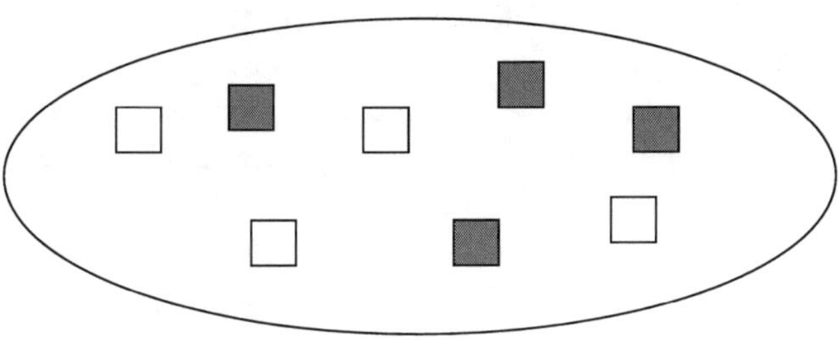

Figure 3: A system with eight elements

$3^8 = 6{,}561$. Allowing each square to have a fourth color would boost the variety to $4^8 = 65{,}536$. It does not take much and the number of possible states reaches enormous heights. Let us now consider the connections between the squares. The number of possible connections is $V = n(n - 1) = 56$. This solution takes into consideration that connections can run both ways and that a connection from A to B is not necessarily the same as from B to A. Still, this is a static system. If the system were dynamic, i. e. if any connection between two squares might be operative or not operative at any time, then the number of possible states would be $V = 2^{56} = 72{,}057{,}594{,}037{,}927{,}936$ which equals roughly 7×10^{16}. All of a sudden, the variety is boosted to astronomical heights. And this is a rather simple system with only eight elements. Now consider the consequences for an ecosystem or the society of the country that you live in. What we realize is that variety proliferates.[30]

Variety proliferation in practice means that a complex system can take on an unimaginable number of possible states. In addition to that, most variables that contribute to creating them are not even known to us, as was mentioned above. It is because of this that complex systems need a different method of handling than simple systems. The central question is:

How can we cope with the potential amount of variety generated in order to keep a complex system under control?

This is not the place for a detailed discussion of variety and its implications.[31] I shall therefore simply state the answer to this question. It was given by the already mentioned British cybernetician W. Ross Ashby: »Only variety can destroy variety.«[32] Or, stating it a bit more neatly:

Only variety absorbs variety.[33]

This is the Law of Requisite Variety, also called Ashby's Law.

To explain what it means I would like to tell the story of how I personally got to understand what Ashby's Law entails. In the late 1990s, I had the pleasure of accompanying my father on a trip to Wales, or more accurately to a place called Cwarel Isaf, which is a cottage not far from the town of Abereron where Elisabeth Taylor and Richard Burton used to hide from Hollywood and the world. Cwarel Isaf was the cottage of Stafford Beer to where he had withdrawn from Chile to study, meditate and write his books in 1973. This had been a consequence of the coup d'état against the Chilean president Salvador Allende, to whom he was an economic counselor from 1971 to 1973. It was a place in the middle of nowhere, down in a little hollow, and persistently cold and damp. The cottage consisted of a bathroom, a bedroom and a living room, which also served as study and kitchen. The only source of heat in this room was a massive iron oven which had to be fired with wood or coal and in front of which my father and I were sitting together with Stafford Beer to discuss his theories – but mostly just to listen to the father of management cybernetics conversing and elaborating. As I was at that time not yet familiar with cybernetics and Stafford Beer's books, I had a tough time trying to follow the conversations and understanding what they were about. However, at one point Stafford seemed to feel sorry for this young lad who had no clue about anything and was freezing to death despite sitting next to the oven. He appeared to want me to understand at least the essential Law of Requisite Variety. So he turned to me and tried to explain Ashby's Law to me. He quickly introduced variety and then said: »Imagine you have a football team of eleven players. How do you keep them under control?« I believe I answered something about ordering them around but I did not really know what to say. So he answered his own question: »By having them play against another football team of eleven players who are about as good as they are. Only variety can absorb variety.«

So what Ashby's Law entails is that you need as much variety yourself as you are confronted with in order have to a system under control. If you do not have requisite variety you need either to amplify your own variety or attenuate the variety out there. In any case, Ashby's law is going to assert itself. If this is to happen without damage, then the system needs to be designed. That is why organization is necessary.

It was also mentioned that we can never know all the details and variables of a complex system – its variety is far too large. Still we need to deal with it – and control it. Obviously, digging down deep and trying to get as much data as possible about the details is the wrong way. We would always end up with insufficient knowledge upon which to base our decisions. What we need to do, then, is to leave the forest so the trees will not block the view anymore and we can actually see it.

Controlling a complex system means focusing on the big picture, on the overall structure. Concerning oneself with the details of the system is the wrong approach. Since we do not know all the details, changing a few will most probably have consequences in areas that we did not foresee. This is what happens in today's politics. You pull a thread and something happens that you did not intend to trigger. Then you are busy fixing things but by doing so you trigger another cascade of unforeseen and undesired events. Before you know it the system is out of control – the exact opposite of what you wished for.

I repeat: control in the cybernetic sense does not mean absolute control of every detail. It is more like steering, directing and guiding. You influence the big picture, the framework, so the system moves in the desired direction. But you have no way of influencing the specifics, the details. They take care of themselves. They self-organize. Still, the system as a whole is under control.

Key to the control of a complex system is organization.[34] We cannot confine a system to certain parameters that we might like. This would maybe attenuate the variety to an amount that we can handle – but it would also kill the system. Take the complexity out of a complex system and you lose the system. Therefore, the only way to regulate a complex system is to organize it. And this finally brings us to Stafford Beer's Viable System Model.

2.2 The Viable System Model

The initial question that led Stafford Beer to the development of the Viable System Model® (VSM®) was: What might be the most sophisticated regulation and control system that nature has devised? His investigation led him

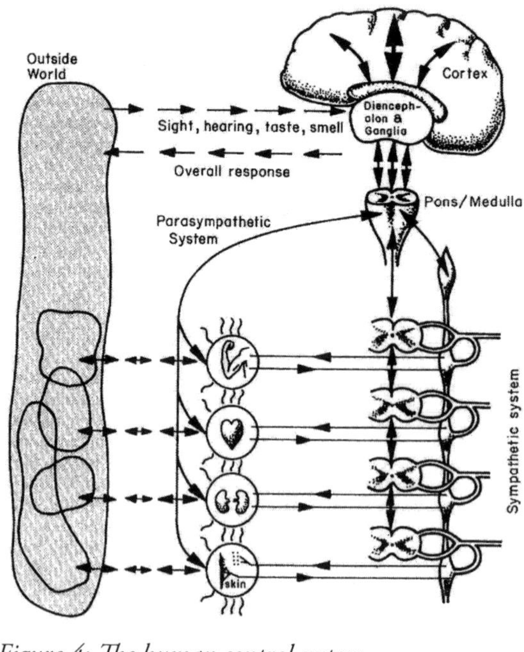

Figure 4: The human control system
Source: Beer, Stafford: Brain of the Firm, 1994.

to the conclusion that it might well be the human central nervous system. Studying and analyzing it, he isolated its fundamental structural characteristics and thereby came up with an abstract model, which is entirely based on structure and independent of content. According to Beer, this model reflects the organization and structure of any system that is supposed to be viable.[35]

I would like to stress that the claim is that any system needs to meet the structural requirements of the model if it is to be viable. Therefore, it does not matter whether this system is the human body, a single celled bacterium, a multi-national enterprise with 50,000 employees or the society of a particular nation. If it lacks one or several of the required components, it is not viable in the long term.

Before we take a closer look at the model, we first need to answer the question: »What is viable?« After all, we can connect a human body to all kinds of machines and thus keep it alive. Or the government can subsidize an entire industry, such as the coal industry in Germany, to keep it from disappearing. But this seems to be stretching the concept of viability. Beer gives the following definition:

Viable means to be able to maintain a separate existence over an undetermined period of time.[36]

It further needs to be noted that the components of the model are necessary but also sufficient for viability.[37] The model, therefore, constitutes the minimum requirement for viability. Furthermore, the model is not supposed to be a recipe to be used in case of emergency. »It is contended that all viable organizations are really like this already. Therefore the value of the model is to make clear how the organization actually works, as distinct from the way it allegedly works, so that it may be streamlined and made more effective.«[38]

We shall discuss the implications and consequences of the model later. Let us now take a look at the model itself.

2.2.1 The Five Subsystems

The structure of the Viable System Model consists of five subsystems, all of which are, as just mentioned, necessary but also sufficient for the viability of a system. There are also certain principles underlying it, with which we shall be dealing later. The elaboration of the model is rather complex and detailed. I shall refrain from repeating it here, as a basic understanding of the model is enough for our purpose. Moreover, I am convinced that the fundamental thought is not that difficult to grasp and that the reader will understand the importance of the model even without in-depth examinations of the individual subsystems and their interconnections.

System 1- The Basic Unit

The basic unit of a viable system is referred to as System 1.[39] It is the Elemental Operational Unit (EOU) of the system and as such »does« what the system is actually supposed to do. In the human body the organs and muscles, for example, constitute a System 1 each. In an enterprise it is usually the departments, and in government it is the ministries. System 1 is where performance takes place. A viable system can, thus, have several Systems 1. Indeed, this will be the rule, but how many there are depends on the system in question.

What is special about a System 1 is that it is itself a viable system. As such it is autonomous within the coherent structure of the overall system. These aspects already refer to the three Principles: Recursion, Autonomy and Viability. The question, therefore, of whether something constitutes a System 1 needs to be based on the consideration of whether it can maintain a separate existence but also of whether it should be able to.

System 1 consists of a Management Unit, an Operational Unit and an Environment. Together they constitute the EOU. Figures 5 and 6 show two ways of depicting an EOU. In reality we find that, as portrayed in Fig-

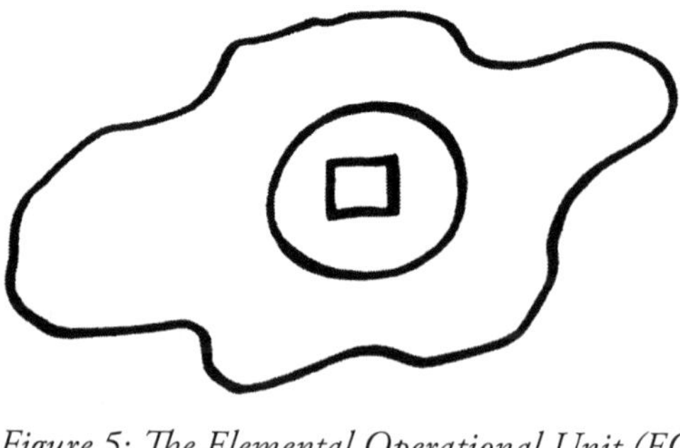

Figure 5: The Elemental Operational Unit (EOU) shown as the Embedment of the Management Unit (square) in the Operational Unit (circle) in the Environment

Source: Beer, Stafford: The Heart of Enterprise, 1994

ure 5, the Management Unit (square) is embedded in the Operational Unit (circle), which is again embedded in the Environment.

This is also a good place to illustrate how variety operates in a system and how variety absorption works. As in any system, there is variety generated in the EOU. In order to show what the relationship in terms of variety is between these three elements, they are taken apart in Figure 6.

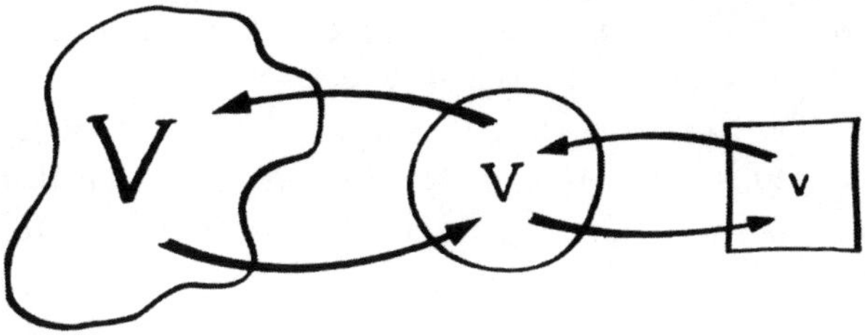

Figure 6: The variety relationsships within the EOU
Source: Beer, Stafford: The Heart of Enterprise, 1994

Now we can see how Ashby's law operates. The Vs in Figure 6 stand for Variety. Each element of the EOU produces a different amount of variety. We can see that the variety of the Environment of System 1 is greater than the one of the Operational Unit, which in turn is greater than the variety of the Management Unit. Between them Ashby's law is operating and, therefore, the Vs tend to equate. This means that variety needs to be either amplified or attenuated (Figure 7).

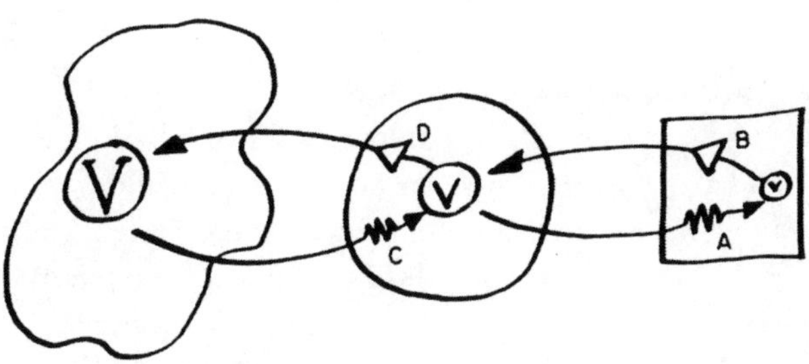

Figure 7: Variety amplification and attenuation in the EOU. Arrows stand for amplification, squiggly lines for attenuation.
Source: Beer, Stafford: The Heart of Enterprise, 1994

There are two possibilities:

The variety on the right-hand side will be amplified in the diffusion process.

The variety on the left-hand side will be attenuated in the diffusion process.

But:

These strategies are not mutually exclusive, and both may be operating.[40]

In any case, Ashby's Law will assert itself and the process of variety absorption needs to be organized so that no damage is caused.

This is to illustrate how the process of variety absorption works. In the following I shall refrain from mentioning it every time. But it is clear that variety absorption processes are constantly at work between any of the subsystems, within them and between the system and its environment.

System 2 – Coordination and Oscillation Damping

We have seen that in a Viable System there will usually be several Systems 1. When drawn on a chart they may look alike, but in reality they may differ substantially. After all, each System 1 is autonomous and has its own business, which operates in an environment peculiar to it. Still, all Systems 1 belong to a greater whole – the Viable System in focus. Therefore, a System 1 should not be operating in a manner which causes trouble to any other System 1. There should be no harmful competition between systems. On the contrary, since they are all part of the same cohesive structure everything should be tried so that synergies will be made use of and the Systems 1 can work together in a constructive and smooth fashion.

To assure that all of this is done is the task of System 2.[41] System 2 coordinates the operations of the Systems 1 and damps possible oscillation. It is important to understand that System 2 does so not by issuing commands. There is no hierarchy in which System 2 might be higher than System 1. All System 2 does is provide a service to System 1. It has a support function. But this support function is extremely important since oscillation occurring in System 1 can easily spread to affect other subsystems thus becoming a problem for the viability of the overall system.

Typical Systems 2 are, for example, the back office staff of a company, the train schedule of a train network, traffic rules and signals such as street lights and stop signs, the air traffic control center of an airport and coordinative regulations between member states of a country such as the tax harmonization law and »interkantonal« treaties in Switzerland.

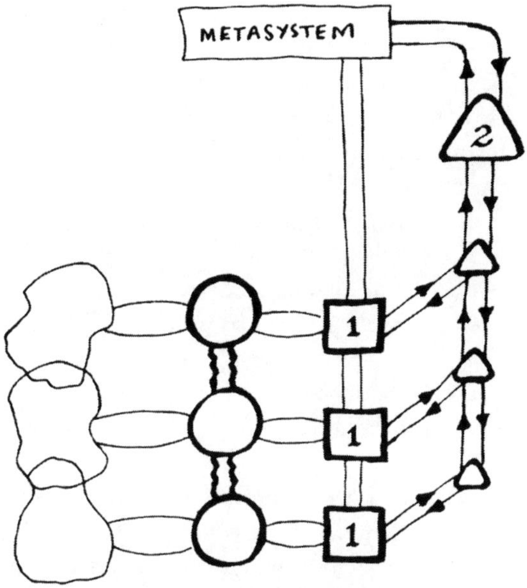

Figure 8: System 2 and its connections to Systems 1 and the meta-system
Source: Beer, Stafford: The Heart of Enterprise, 1994

System 3 – Operative Management

System 1 is the system through which the Viable System achieves its purpose. As there usually are several Systems 1, there needs to be a System 2 for coordination and oscillation damping. However, this is not enough. In addition to this, a system is required which fulfills a regulative and steering function for the sake of the cohesion of the whole. The Systems 1 need to operate in the light of the purpose of the overall Viable System and someone needs to make sure that this is achieved.

This is the purpose of System 3, which is also called operative management.[42] It is responsible for System 1 operating within the scope of the purpose of the Viable System and being cohesive with its structure. Furthermore, it is responsible for the allocation of resources to System 1 such as money, time and people but also for example IT support and legal services. In short, System 3 needs to make sure that System 1 gets what it needs to fulfill its task within the limits and for the sake of the Viable System as a whole. The government of a country or the management of a company are typical examples.

To fulfill its purpose System 3 necessarily needs to be able to issue commands to System 1. However, this command channel should be used as rarely and as subtly as possible. The reason is the variety created in System 1. Although there is a constant flow of information from System 1 to System 3, only System 1 possesses all the information that is needed to cope with the variety created in its environment. That is why it needs to be autonomous within the cohesive structure of the overall system.[43] If System 3 were to make excessive use of its power to issue commands, it would strangle this autonomy, which would then result in an inability of System 1 to make full use of the knowledge it possesses to cope with its own variety. And System 3 does not have requisite variety to do so in its stead. Therefore, the better System 1 has been set up and the better the coordination by System 2 works, the less System 3 will have to issue direct commands to restrain the autonomy of System 1.

For System 3 to be able to regulate everything for the sake of the cohesion and the purpose of the overall Viable System, it needs to have the right information about what is happening in System 1. In Figure 8 the connections between Systems 1, 2 and 3 are shown (System 3 is part of the meta-system). It can be seen that System 3 receives information from the Management Units of System 1 and from System 2 as well. This information, however, is

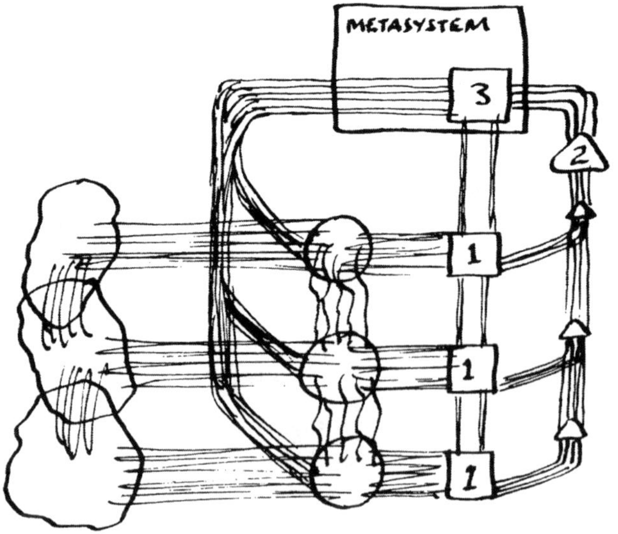

Figure 9: System 3 and its connections to Systems 1 and 2
Source: Beer, Stafford: The Heart of Enterprise, 1994

filtered. It is not information from the »frontline« if you will. But information of this sort, which is unfiltered, is necessary for System 3 to be able to put the filtered information that it obtains into context. That is why we can see, in Figure 9, a direct information channel from System 3 to the Operational Units of System 1.

The channels from System 3 to the Management Units and to System 2 alone are not able to transport requisite variety. The sole use of these channels would only lead to the above-discussed overloading of the command line, which would result in the loss of autonomy of System 1 – and in autocracy. That is why the link between the operations of System 1 and System 3 is necessary (Figures 10 and 11).

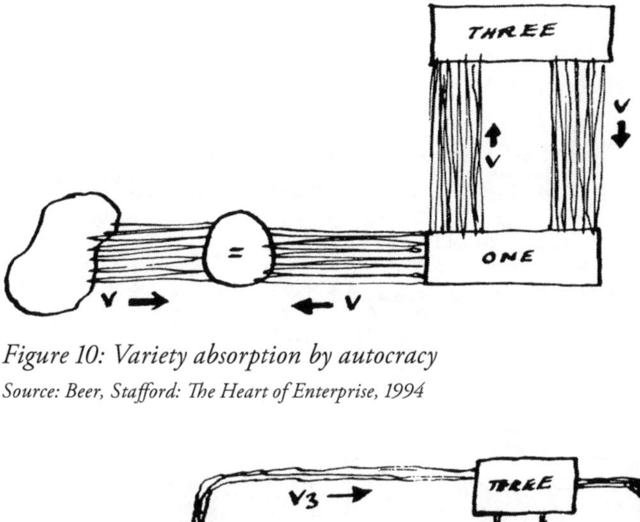

Figure 10: Variety absorption by autocracy
Source: Beer, Stafford: The Heart of Enterprise, 1994

Figure 11: Variety absorption by autonomy
Source: Beer, Stafford: The Heart of Enterprise, 1994

System 3 concerns itself with what is going on within the system. It sees to it that things on the inside are stable and smooth. Moreover, its concern is the present. It regulates things now, it issues commands for present actions and it allocates recourses for present projects. That is why Beer's motto for System 3 was inside and now. However, a system that means to be viable needs to be concerned about external things and things to come as well.

System 4 – Strategic Management

A system needs to be able to cope with things that come from the outside and it needs to be able to adjust to changed circumstances as they might present themselves in the future. System 3 cannot do this as it is busy looking at the inside and now. Therefore, another system is needed, which concerns itself with what is outside the Viable System and in the future. This is the task of System 4 and this task involves more or less everything that is dubbed »strategic« nowadays.[44]

Beer called the focus of System 4 the outside and then. This illustrates that System 4 needs to look at an environment which necessarily encompasses more than just the sum of the environments of System 1. It needs to ask the question of what kind of environment might be important to the system's survival tomorrow. It is the risks and chances that the system might

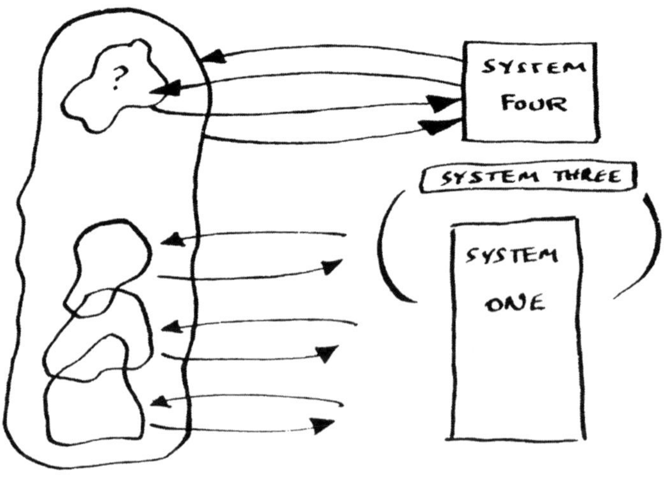

Figure 12: System 4 – a larger environment and an unknown future
Source: Beer, Stafford: The Heart of Enterprise, 1994

encounter in the future which are the main concern of System 4. Examples of System 4 include research and development departments, earthquake surveillance systems or intelligence agencies.

Whereas System 3 ensures the short-term survival of the system here and now, System 4 needs to make sure the system is prepared for tomorrow's developments and does not go blindly into the future. Its focus is the long term.

This fundamentally different perspective of Systems 3 and 4 will often lead to frictions between these two systems. They do not understand their respective worlds and will always try to stress the importance of their own point of view. But for the Viable System both approaches are indispensable for its survival and, therefore, one last system is needed to supervise the interaction of Systems 3 and 4.

System 5 – Normative Management

The task of System 5 is what you could call normative management.[45] It has to balance the actions and perspectives of Systems 3 and 4 – present and future, inside and outside – and use them for the benefit of the overall system.

System 5 provides what cybernetics calls closure. As feedback is a core concept in cybernetics, systems on the whole need feedback about themselves, too. Information produced by the system needs to be fed back into

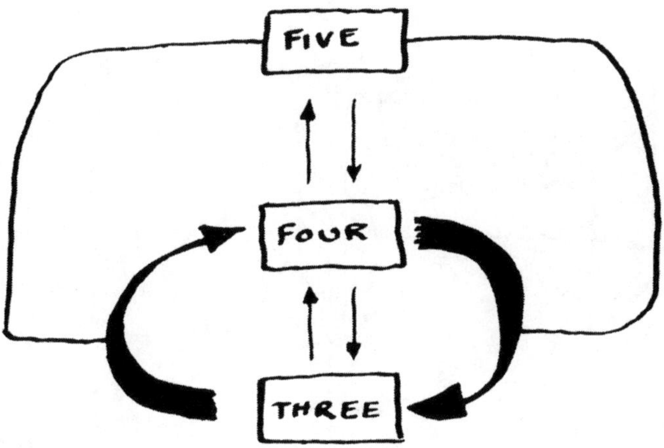

Figure 13: System 5 and its monitoring task of the 3–4 interaction
Source: Beer, Stafford: The Heart of Enterprise, 1994

the system to provide self-reference. This is what closure does. It provides self-reference. Therefore, closure is not something that blocks off information and influences from the outside world and keeps the system to itself: »... by ›closure‹ I mean a self-referential process, and not the isolation of the system within an adiabatic shell.«[46] By obtaining self-reference thanks to the concept of closure, the system gains identity.

The constitution of a country is part of System 5, as is the board of directors of a company. In a family, the parents constitute System 5, and in the human being an important System 5-function is assumed by what we call conscience.

The model

Figure 14 shows the model of the Viable System in its entirety with the various connections between the five subsystems illustrating the variety flow. Three things need to be mentioned in addition to the explanations of the sub-systems for a correct understanding of the drawing.

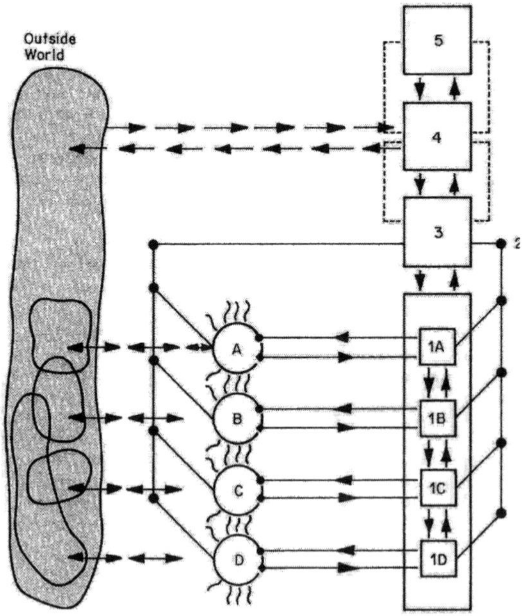

Figure 14: The Viable System Model
Source: Beer, Stafford: Brain of the Firm, 1994

First, the different environments have a variable shape similar to that of an amoeba. This is to show that they do not have fixed boundaries. On the one hand, it is difficult to tell where the relevant environment for a system ends in the first place. It is, therefore, important to keep in mind that one needs to question one's definition of the environment continuously as it is always subjective to a certain extent. On the other hand, as circumstances change, so does an environment. Thus, the boundaries of an environment are in flux and the system needs to take this into account.[47]

Second, the squiggly lines between the Operational Units of System 1 depict informal connections between these Units. Although all the Systems 1 of a Viable System are autonomous and limited in their autonomy only for the sake of the cohesion of the overall structure, and although coordination is organized by System 2, it would be erroneous to believe that the Systems 1 are not somehow in touch with each other and are ignorant of one another. There is always some kind of exchange between them no matter how subtle it may be. Indeed, the connections between the Operational Units are important because they absorb variety which otherwise would have to be coped with by other channels within the structure of the Viable System.[48]

Third, Systems 3, 4 and 5 constitute a meta-system within the overall structure. They are meta to Systems 1 and 2. This does not simply mean that they are hierarchically higher. First and foremost they are logically higher. This means that the meta-system speaks a different language for it deals with a different sort of information, with different variables and different aspects of the system.[49] System 1 is concerned with the question of what is necessary to operate successfully. System 2 coordinates the various efforts of the several Systems 1 but it is still on the same level. Systems 3, 4 and 5, however, are concerned with the cohesion of the whole Viable System and, therefore, need to address issues which are altogether different from those addressed by Systems 1 and 2. The meta-system consisting of the Systems 3, 4 and 5 »… is a collection of subsystems that exists to look after the collection of operational elements, so that they cohere in that totality which we called a viable system. … Whatever is needed to manage the collection of operational elements is METASYSTEMIC to that. It is something logically beyond (that is, meta) the logic of the operational elements combined.«[50]

The structure of the Viable System Model is invariant. This means that no matter what kind of system we are referring to and no matter in what kind of environment it is applied the five subsystem structure remains unchanged – if the system means to be viable. The model constitutes a structural pattern for viability. The word pattern needs to be stressed, for the

VSM can be compared to a vessel whose shape remains constant but whose content changes depending on the system. So in reality we need to have the pattern in our head when we approach a system. We will find numerous elements to which we then need to apply the structural pattern of the VSM. If we change the system, the elements change – but the pattern remains. The VSM helps identify strengths and weaknesses of the organization of any system. »Therefore the value of the model is to make clear how the organization actually works, as distinct from the way it allegedly works, so that it may be streamlined and made more effective.«[51]

What remains for us to look at now are three principles that are fundamental to the model and its understanding.

2.2.2 Principles

The three fundamental principles that underlie the Viable System Model have already briefly been mentioned in connection with the characteristics of System 1. We shall discuss them now in greater detail, as a more profound understanding of the model is not possible without any knowledge of these principles.

The Principle of Recursion

It was said that System 1 is itself a Viable System. This is the case because the entire model takes on a recursive structure. Recursiveness means that the structure of the model is the same on each level of observation, i. e. level of recursion. So if a given Viable System is level 3 of the recursive structure, then its Systems 1 would be Viable Systems with the same five-subsystem structure on recursion level 4, and their respective Systems 1 would be Viable Systems in turn on level 5. The same would hold true in the other direction: Our Viable System constituting recursion level 3 would be a System 1 of the Viable System on recursion level 2 which in turn is a System 1 on recursion level 1. We can, therefore, say that any Viable System contains and is contained in another Viable System. The structure on each level of recursion is invariant – the pattern remains the same. Beer has actually given us two possible variations of the principle of recursion:

»If a viable system contains a viable system, then the organizational structure must be recursive.«[52]

»If we decide to define a social system by recursion we shall find that every viable system contains a viable system.«[53]

The model, therefore, is not hierarchical in the way that we usually use the word. Looking at one level of recursion isolated from the rest it actually is since the meta-system is placed above the other system's components. But if we take more than one level of recursion into consideration then it becomes clear that it is not hierarchical in the usual sense. It is rather a structure in which each system is »nested« in another system. A system hereby is embedded in the system of one higher level of recursion. And the relationship between them is not simply hierarchical but rather logically graded – the higher system is logically higher, meta to the lower one.

It is, for several reasons, not easy to show this recursive structure on a two-dimensional graph.[54] But Figure 15 tries to make clear how the »nesting« of two levels of recursion is supposed to be understood.

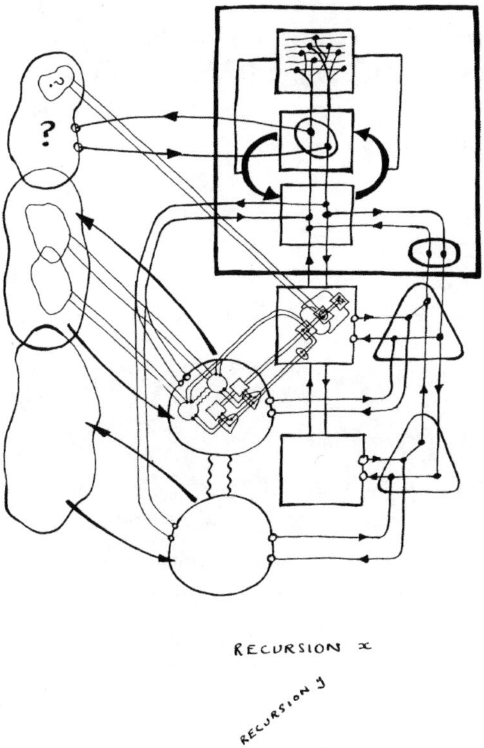

Figure 15: Two levels of recursion of the Viable System
Source: Beer, Stafford: The Heart of Enterprise, 1994

The principle of recursion cannot be properly understood without the principle of viability because it is crucial that each level of recursion refers to a Viable System and not just to any system one would like to see as a level of recursion.[55] Central to the concept of recursion is the viability of the system as defined by the model of the Viable System on each level of recursion.

The recursive structure of the system allows us to have a model of a complex system, which provides as much variety as the complex system itself. And, as cybernetics teaches, this is absolutely necessary if we are to use the model as reference for possible steering and control measures.

Furthermore, according to Malik the recursive nature of the model offers several other advantages:[56]

1. The systems on each level of recursion are all entities in the systemic sense as they exhibit all the structural elements of the Viable System.
2. Each system of this kind has a high potential for coping with complexity as it has a certain autonomy and independence.
3. Because of the recursiveness of the structure it is possible to have, on each level of recursion, the same mind set, methods, techniques, programs and structural principles for the detailed specifics of the system. This leads to an improvement of the possible variety design and, hence, to notable rationalizations.
4. A random design of the structure of a system is not possible anymore due to the criteria given by the Viable System Model. The criteria can therefore be objectively discussed for the first time. This makes the Viable System Model a valuable tool for the diagnosis and the design of a system.

The Principle of Autonomy

A System 1 as a viable system is to be given the greatest possible autonomy and independence by the meta-system together with which it constitutes the Viable System of the next level of recursion. This autonomy is to be restricted only for the sake of the cohesion of the overall system. Other than that, the Systems 1, i. e. the Viable Systems of the next lower level of recursion, have the liberty to take action and behave as they think appropriate.

Beer's definition of autonomy is as follows:

»If a system regulates itself by subtracting at all times as little horizontal variety as is necessary to maintain the cohesion of the total system, then the condition of autonomy prevails.«[57]

This question is directly linked with the question of centralization and decentralization. Commonly, the concepts of centralization and decentralization are considered to be two extremes of a horizontal scale and, as neither is desirable, the solution is searched somewhere in the middle (Figure 16).

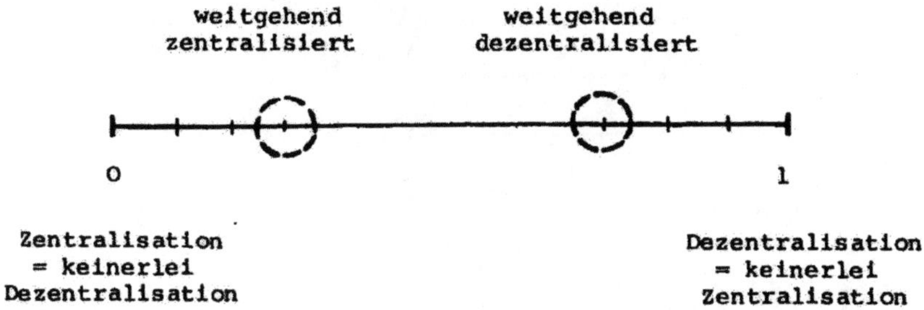

Figure 16: Classical interpretation of the centralization-decentralization problem
Source: Malik, Fredmund: Strategie des Managements komplexer Systeme, 2003

Cybernetic research, however, has proven that at least two dimensions are needed for a serious discussion of the problem. On the horizontal axis there are the several subsystems as fundamentally autonomous systems. The vertical axis represents the authority of the meta-system to induce or restrict a particular behavior of the individual subsystems (Figure 17).[58]

There are two kinds of possible interventions by the meta-system:[59] There can be a selection process between the different Systems 1. Certain actions of the selected System 1 can be allowed or prohibited. The meta-system is therefore responsible for two things:

- The autonomy of the individual Systems 1.
- The cohesion of the overall structure of the Viable System in focus.

Autonomy does not mean »laisser faire«. It means balancing authority by the meta-system for the sake of the whole with the independence of the viable sub-systems. The standard always needs to be the cohesion of the overall system. This might sound simple, but in practice it will often be difficult to decide which measures serve this overall cohesion and which ones restrict the autonomy of the subsystems in an improper way.

Today's politics are a useful negative example. There is a clear overuse of the command channel in practically all countries. Over-regulation in all areas and government interference in far too many matters strangle the liberty of elements which should actually be given much more independence and

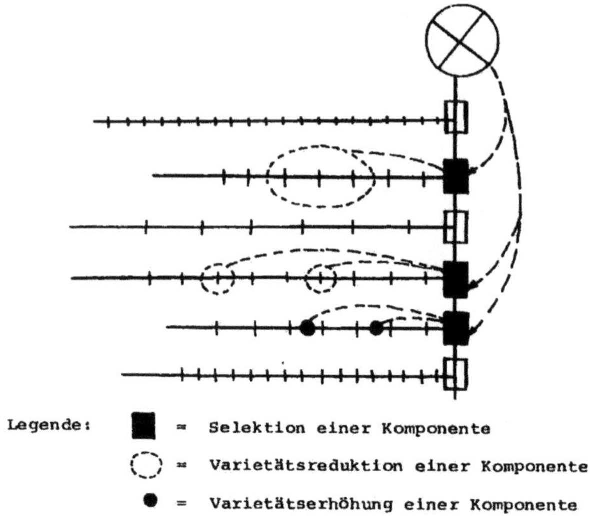

Figure 17: Cybernetic interpretation of the centralization-decentralization problem (with the square representing the selection of a component, the dotted circle variety reduction, and the black circle showing increases in variety)
Source: Malik, Fredmund: Strategie des Managements komplexer Systeme, 2003

autonomy, such as the member states of a country. Thereby variety, which should and could have been absorbed on System-1 level, spreads to the meta-system, which does not have requisite variety to deal with it. Countries such as Switzerland, the United States or Canada with an explicit and distinctive federal organization are better off, but even in these states the federal government assumes responsibility for more and more things which should actually remain with the member states.

The Principle of Viability

A lot has been said already about viability. The definition is clear:

Viable means to be able to maintain a separate existence over an undetermined period of time.[60]

Here, it needs to be stressed again that this abstract concept of viability does not tell us anything about the specifics of a system. It is a statement about a configuration of states that can be upheld over an undetermined period of time. Now, there might be several such lasting configurations that range from bare survival to prosperity.[61] Which ones are lasting and which ones are not, and which of the lasting ones will, moreover, lead the system to prosperity is something that needs to be found out in each individual case.

The Viable System Model with its five-subsystem structure gives us a tool to assess the structural and systemic efficiency of a system.[62] Without the model's structural pattern a system can never be viable in the above-mentioned sense. Viability is therefore a meta-criterion.[63] The fundamental question needs to be whether a system fulfills the requirements of the Viable System Model. All other measures and actions are of secondary importance.

I would like to remind the reader once more that the principle of viability needs to be met on all levels of recursion. We cannot design the overall system as a Viable System and forget about the Systems 1. The recursiveness of the model entails that the different levels of recursion are interconnected. For example, a System 1 with an insufficient structure will supply the meta-system with the wrong kind of information, which will then be harmful to the overall system. Every system on every level of recursion needs to be able to maintain a separate existence over an undetermined period of time.

2.3 Conclusions

The social systems that we live in, and especially society itself, are complex systems. A wrong kind of understanding of these systems and a plan of action to control them based on such a wrong understanding will eventually have disastrous consequences. Ashby's Law will always assert itself and it does not care whether we care about it or not. Variety operates at all times whether we recognize it or not. To prevent it from causing any damage to people and assets, the organizational structure of our systems needs to be designed properly.[64] For this we need to know how complex systems work and how they can be controlled. Cybernetics as the science of the control of complex systems can help us with this. The current classical reductionist approaches that still cling to the concept of control in the sense of controlling every detail and specific do not only not offer any help but actually make things worse.

Beer's Viable System Model provides the possibility of diagnosing and structuring a system properly so that we are in control of it in the cybernetic sense. This means that we no longer take action ignorant of the actual mechanisms that are at work. The measures taken are not »blind« anymore, if you will.

We need society to be stable in the sense of cybernetically viable, if peace and order and freedom are to prevail. It needs to be able to be flexible and adaptable to new internal and external influences. The Viable System Model tells us how society needs to be organized to achieve this goal.

In this book we ask the question of whether it is not possible for legislative bodies to anticipate future developments to help society adapt and adjust in order for it not to be crushed by certain events and their consequences. During the discussion of the five subsystems of the Viable System Model the reader will certainly already have realized that for this purpose System 4 plays a decisive role, as it is concerned with the outside and then of a system. It explicitly asks the question of what future developments the system will have to cope with in order to survive.

In Part IV of this book we will be looking more closely at the consequences that the Model of the Viable System and especially System 4 have for our question, as we will try to make certain suggestions as to the organization of legislative bodies. However, before we do so we first need to examine in greater detail the source of the phenomena mentioned in Part I, which can lead to the destabilization of society – we need to examine the crowd. In the course of this examination a theory will be introduced – the new theory of Socionomics –, which we will be able to use as a tool within System 4 of the Viable System Model to directly anticipate future events and developments.

Part III – Anticipation

3. Crowd Psychology and Socionomics

3.1 Crowd Psychology

3.1.1 The mirage of the dominance of human rationality

Man creates society. But he does so rationally – and even knowingly – only to a certain extent. Today we are taught to believe that what we see around us is the product of human will and reason. It is common doctrine that the achievements of civilization be it arts, the economy, our legal system or political institutions have been designed deliberately by man for man. In our current view there is still only very little room for accident and coincidence or for the concept of the evolution of social systems.

The origins of this notion which, following Friedrich von Hayek, I shall call constructivistic rationalism[65], can be traced to the great French thinker René Descartes. To Descartes, reason meant the logical deduction from explicit premises, and he therefore accepted as true only those arguments, conclusions and propositions that had been reached in this way.[66]

Subsequently, Descartes' followers applied his idea, which he himself had only used for philosophical considerations, to actions and, as a consequence, only such actions came to be accepted as rational that were based on demonstrable truth in the Cartesian sense. This led to the erroneous conclusion that only actions that were true in this sense could be regarded as good and useful actions, and that everything else, everything »irrational«, could lead to any benefit for the human being. It was for this reason that tradition and history came to be thought of as unnecessary and were rejected as sources of human culture. Reason alone was supposed to enable the individual to assume responsibility for his future and lead to progress and prosperity.[67]

This is not the place to explain in detail the tenets and consequences of the constructivistic approach. A brilliant treatise upon this can be found in Friedrich von Hayek's *Law, Legislation and Liberty.* I mention it here simply because it is important to see that this approach, which has been dominating our thinking for more than three hundred years, is wrong in that it falls short of what actually happens in our world.

It is not just man's ability of rational thinking that shapes society. There are also other forces at work that are beyond anyone's ability to control. These forces are far older than man and he is still subject to them. Without taking them into account, full comprehension of our world is not possible.

The supporters of that other kind of rationalism, which is called critical rationalism and of which, for example, Sir Karl Popper and Hans Albert are two of the prominent representatives, have always been well aware of that. Constructivistic rationalism is only concerned with what the ancient Greeks called *taxis,* a man-made order. It does not acknowledge the fact that these man-made, designed orders are only a part of reality. It is very likely that most of the achievements of human culture have never been deliberately and consciously designed. They have grown. They are not *taxis* but *cosmos*[68], a grown order; they are, as Adam Ferguson put it, the result of human action but not of human design.[69]

The constructivistic approach reflects man's inclination to look at things anthropomorphically and interpreting his environment in this manner. Religion with its God figure and its concept of creation certainly plays a major part in this, too. It is therefore not surprising that the constructivistic followers fall victim to what has been called the synoptic delusion[70] and suggest that behind cultural and social achievements there must be a mind – be it a divine being or merely man – to which they are due.

Two things are important with respect to this. First, it is inappropriate to believe that our brain was fully developed before there was culture or society. It is wrong to assume that our brain, our mind developed its full capacity first and that this in turn enabled us to create society deliberately and rationally. It was most probably a common and joint process in which culture and brain fostered their respective developments. There is no reason to believe that mind was there before culture, which in turn owes its existence to the former.

»Mind is as much the product of the social environment in which it has grown up and which it has not made as something that has in turn acted upon and altered these institutions. It is the result of man having developed in society and having acquired those habits and practices that increased the chances of persistence of the group in which he lived. The conception of an already fully developed mind designing the institutions, which made life in society possible, is contrary to all we know about the evolution of man.«[71]

Second, there is no mind that could ever know all the facts that are necessary to design a system as complex as our society. The systems sciences and complexity theory have long proven that it is impossible to know all the variables that contribute to a complex system and that, therefore, it is impossible to control all the details of such a system.[72] A complex system is a cosmos. It grows and evolves due to knowledge that only its individual elements possess[73] and due to rules and behavioral patterns that have developed over hundreds of thousands of years and are deeply ingrained.

In such an evolving system there is only so much room for rational behavior. On the one hand, we are restricted by handed-down rules of just conduct, as Hayek calls them, that have developed over thousands of generations. Tradition has been playing a key part in our society until this day. On the other hand, we still follow instincts and behavioral patterns that go back to times when man did not yet exist. We share such instincts with animals[74] and, despite the fact that we are now qualified by reason, a much more sophisticated tool, we are still frequently slaves to these pre-human inbuilt mechanisms.

3.1.2 The other-directedness of people[75]

One such instinct – and an extremely important one – that has survived in us from earlier times is the tendency among people to orient themselves on what others do and the tendency to herd and flock. Today, as we focus on reason and logic, scientific theories in all fields also concentrate on the individual because only in the individual can there be reason in the Cartesian sense.[76] The individual is at the core of society and it is the individual's rationality which is the driving force of society. This is the dominant view today.

That this is so can best be seen in the field of economics. Here the Efficient Markets Hypothesis (EMH) with its *homo oeconomicus* is still the state of the art, and the individual and its rationality are at its center. EMH states that individuals make decisions rationally and independently based only on their own personal preferences, wishes and needs.[77] It treats individuals as something detached from the environment they exist in as if all a man needs were himself and his reason. It is following EMH and based on the homo oeconomicus conception of man that economists all over the world analyze markets and give counsel to political leaders.

In recent years, the *homo oeconomicus* concept has been increasingly challenged. W. Brian Arthur of Stanford University and the Santa Fe Institute writes:

»If we were to imagine the vast collection of decision problems economic agents might conceivably deal with as a sea or an ocean, with the easier problems on top and more complicated ones at increasing depth, then deductive rationality would describe human behavior accurately only within a few feet of the surface. ... The level at which humans can apply perfect rationality is surprisingly modest.«[78]

And Amos Tversky and Daniel Kahneman call the assumption of rationality »a self-evident truth, a reasonable idealization, a tautology, and a null hypothesis«.[79] It was especially the »behavioral» disciplines, of which Kahneman is one of the most prominent representatives today, such as Behavioral Economics, Behavioral Finance and Behavioral Law that have started to question the rigid concept of *homo oeconomicus* by including psychological insights and asking how »real people« differ from the homo oeconomicus.[80] Behavioral Economics has become an established and recognized science as was demonstrated by the fact that the Nobel Prize for Economics was awarded to Daniel Kahneman in 2002.[81] Despite this, EMH remains the prominent view.

Admittedly, EMH is a beautiful theory because it is so simple, yet it is wrong because of that. The human being is not that simple. He is a complex system himself to whose behavior diverse variables contribute of which reason is but one. And to look at man without looking at his environment at the same time is wrong in the first place. The system in focus must always be the system in its environment.[82]

An important part of the environment of a person is other people. Humans are no loners. Man is a social being that constantly interacts with his fellow citizens and is influenced by what goes on around him. It is true that people often make decisions based on their own knowledge and their own preferences. But it is also true that very often they do not. In many situations people will turn to others to find out what it is that they should do. David Riesman, the author of *The Lonely Crowd*, writes:

»What is common to all the other-directed people is that their contemporaries are the source of direction for the individual – either those known to him or those with whom he is indirectly acquainted, through friends and through the mass media.«[83]

The others are an extremely important source of information and any theory concerned with trying to explain human decision-making processes and indeed human behavior in general needs to take this into account.[84]

3.1.3 Crowds – man in masses

The other-directedness is a concept that has emerged from the study of crowds. So far there have been relatively few such studies and it has been only recently that science started increasingly to acknowledge and analyze crowd phenomena. Still, crowds and their dynamics are as yet far from being understood. Peter Drucker writes:

»Surely no discovery or invention of this century has had greater impact than the social innovation of mass and mass movement. Yet none is less understood. Indeed, in respect to the mass we are today pretty much where we were in respect to the psychodynamics of the individual a hundred years ago.«[85]

I believe it is the insight into the limits of the conventional approaches that has fostered the realization of the importance of crowds, for it is increasingly becoming clear that man and society cannot be adequately explained without the attempt to understand the behavior of crowds. The reason for this is, firstly, that crowd phenomena have a large impact on societal development, as they are the driving force behind many of them, and, secondly, that they cannot be explained by focusing on the individual and then simply multiplying its behavior as soon as large numbers of individuals are involved. Crowds, as we shall see, follow laws of their own. They have characteristics that are distinct from those of the individuals that they are composed of.[86]

Moreover, crowd psychology has always tended to focus on crimes committed on a large scale. It was mainly in times of war, revolution and genocide that crowds found their way into people's consciousness and it was mostly in connection with history's great seducers such as Napoleon or Hitler. When people think of a crowd they think of a mob. I believe it is because of this that consideration of crowds and their behavior has largely been viewed as something »ugly« or »filthy« and studies have mainly been conducted concerning the crimes committed by crowds.[87]

Yet, the criminal aspect is only one aspect of crowds. Just as someone's sins and vices do not sum up their personality, mass crimes are only one facet of the »crowd soul«.[88] Crowds can be criminal, but they can also be heroic. It depends on the end towards which a crowd is directed.[89] And often crowds will have an impact that cannot be fitted into categories of good and evil.

There is one more aspect that is worth mentioning, which has, in my opinion, greatly contributed to the disregard of crowds in modern theories. Our western societies are founded on the basis of the concept of free will and self-responsibility of the individual. This concept is jeopardized by crowd psychological insights, as it is not man's free will and reason but his unconscious and instinctive side that is in control in a crowd. This necessarily leads to conflicts with our conception of man and to legal problems, especially in criminal law, as it raises the question as to the actions for which someone can actually be held responsible. Moreover, it simply creates an uneasy feeling if we need to assume that our will is quite often not as free as we might think and like. I believe that this has led many scholars to ignore crowds and focus on the individual. The issue of crowds and free will certainly will have to concern us in the future, but it is not the topic of this book and will have to be covered somewhere else.

It must be made clear here that the crowd phenomena that we see are only part of the phenomena that actually occur. They are the visible, the obvious ones but there are others, invisible ones. Revolutions and mass panics are only the ones that are on the surface, if you will, and that is why they come to our attention. Beneath the surface crowds are at work all the time – more subtly and not as violently – but influencing and shaping society nevertheless. These two kinds of crowds can perhaps be compared to the waves of the ocean. The ones that break, the ones with a white crest, are the ones that attract our attention. Yet the long and less violent waves are at least as important. They are there all the time shaping and defining the character of the sea.

As we shall be more concerned with the latter category of crowds, it might be, nonetheless, useful to have a quick look at crowds in general. On the one hand, this should give an impression of and a feeling for what crowds are and how they behave. On the other hand, visible crowd phenomena (or advanced or second order phenomena as I shall call them) often result from invisible ones (basic or first order phenomena) or at least could not occur without them. Understanding crowds in general might make it easier to make the link between them and then see why the study of basic crowd movements is so relevant.

The crowd

One of the essential features of a crowd, as we usually see it, if not the defining and constituent feature, is the fact that individuals within a crowd do not behave individually anymore or only in a very limited way. They are sucked in by the crowd and follow nothing but its dynamics. That is why the characteristics of the crowd cannot or can only inadequately be explained by looking at the individual. Something new comes into being with rules and behavioral patterns of its own that absorbs individuality and transforms it into conformity. In the preface to his book »The Crowd: A Study of the Popular Mind« Gustave Le Bon, one of the fathers of crowd psychology, already states as early as 1911:

»When, however, a certain number of these individuals are gathered together in a crowd for purposes of action, observation proves that, from the mere fact of their being assembled, there result certain new psychological characteristics, which are added to the racial characteristics and differ from them at times to a very considerable degree.«[90]

And Peter F. Drucker writes: »The mass is a collective. It has a behavior of its own and an identity of its own. … The essence of the mass movement is concentration.«[91] Le Bon speaks in this context of »la loi de l'unité mentale des foules«,[92] the law of the mental unity of crowds. He further accurately states that a gathering of individuals (note: not necessarily a geographical one!) forms a crowd only under certain circumstances. Thus, not always is a number of people also a crowd in the sense mentioned above.[93]

It is, therefore, important to ask when a crowd starts being a crowd or, in other words, what it is that makes a crowd. The question is up to what point it is not yet useful to speak of a crowd but merely of a gathering of people who do not follow any kind of common internal dynamics. For example, it would probably not be appropriate to speak of a crowd when referring to a loose bunch of people in a supermarket who by mere accident find themselves in the same place to go about the same kind of business. However, this loose bunch of individuals might be transformed into a crowd when a fire erupts and a panic breaks out. In between there are different scenarios imaginable that might not easily be defined as one or the other. The transition from one state to the other is probably rather fluid. A situation may often be in the balance and which way it will tilt will depend on the circumstances and the elements.

The number of people involved most probably plays a rather unimportant role in defining a crowd. Le Bon states: »At certain moments half a dozen men might constitute a psychological crowd, which may not happen in the case of hundreds of men gathered together by accident.«[94] Half a dozen is probably not quite enough to establish a crowd. At this number we are still in the realm of the group which has its own dynamics. But the boundary is fluent. In any case, the circumstances and the elements play the decisive role. They are more important than the number of people involved.

Morphology of crowds

Before we talk about the characteristics that all crowds have in common, it might be useful to look at a possible categorization of crowd phenomena. Several attempts have already been made to come up with categories of crowds in order to understand and handle them better.

Le Bon divides crowds into heterogeneous crowds and homogenous crowds. Heterogeneous crowds can be subdivided into anonymous crowds such as a mob in the street and non-anonymous crowds such as court juries and representatives in parliament. Homogenous crowds would be sects, castes and social classes.[95]

Sigmund Freud sees many ways of differentiating between particular crowds but stresses the difference between crowds with leaders and those without leaders.[96]

William McDougall focuses on the degree of organization of a crowd and differentiates between four stages of organization, which go from an »unorganized mob« to groups of »continued existence« with an »elaborate and definite organization«.[97]

Elias Canetti sees three different pairs of crowds: open and closed, rhythmical and stagnant, slow and quick crowds and then differentiates according to the guiding emotion a crowd displays between baiting crowds, flight crowds, prohibition crowds, reversal crowds and feast crowds.[98]

I believe that any of these categorizations is justified depending on what aspect of a crowd one considers the most vital. I shall not go into the details of these distinctions because, for our purpose, I would like to propose a different categorization: namely that into first and second order crowd phenomena, or in more simple words, basic and advanced crowd phenomena. This is, if you will, a combination of the categorizations of McDougall and Canetti with some additional considerations. I have chosen this distinction mainly for three reasons which help us distinguish between first and second order crowds: firstly, the concept of critical mass and discharge; secondly, that of long and short waves; and thirdly, the distinction between crowds and crowd phenomena.

Critical mass and discharge

There are certain characteristics that can almost always be found in second order crowd phenomena but that occur either not at all or only to a very limited degree in first order crowd phenomena. Most studies so far have focused on advanced crowd phenomena and it has been possible to identify their specifics quite accurately. Two are in my opinion especially important: the concept of critical mass and what Elias Canetti calls »Entladung«, discharge.

When the number of people involved in a crowd movement exceeds a certain limit the process becomes somewhat automated. People become drawn to the movement more and more rapidly if not exponentially and the process becomes self-sustaining.[99] It can be compared to reactions in chemistry or physics, where a process becomes self-sustaining and automatic as soon as enough outside energy has been introduced so two substances can react with one another. In crowd psychology, the term used for this limit is critical mass. Social scientists have adopted this term from nuclear engineering.[100]

The concept of »Entladung«, discharge, is closely related to that of critical mass. In fact, it is the reaching of the critical mass that triggers the discharge although often a catalyst of some sort is involved.[101] Canetti calls it the moment when all that belong to a crowd lose their differences and feel the same. According to Canetti, the discharge is what really constitutes a crowd; prior to the discharge it did not yet actually exist.[102]

Critical mass and discharge are peculiar to second order crowd phenomena. They do not occur in basic crowd movements. There is no such thing as exponential or self-sustaining growth in first order phenomena. They are much slower and less violent, which is why they are not usually noticed as crowd phenomena. However, as we shall see, they are driven by the same mechanism as second order phenomena: mental contagion, imitation and emulation are at their root just as much as they are the source of advanced processes. Whenever a critical mass and a discharge occur in a basic crowd phenomenon, it transforms into an advanced one, which leads us to the second of our three points.

Long and short waves

First order phenomena are often the basis for second order ones. Not always will a basic crowd phenomenon give birth to one of second order. It might swell and then ebb away just like the tide without creating any breakers. But sometimes it will reach the critical mass that is necessary to create an advanced phenomenon.

It must be added that there are advanced movements that occur without any underlying basic ones. A panic is a typical example. Clearly, there is nothing underneath it since it is caused by some sudden outside event. But most of the time at least a shared mood, being a first order phenomenon, will be the source of second order processes and that phenomenon itself is then simply a manifestation of that mood.[103]

Crowds versus crowd phenomena

The third reason why I propose to draw a distinction between basic and advanced crowd phenomena is that the former are actually crowds of a lesser degree. It has been said that unity of mind is probably the constituting characteristic of a crowd. Now, the extent to which first order crowds possess this characteristic is far smaller than with second order crowds. For a second order crowd the direction or goal will be the primary focus and most other things will be of secondary importance. In first order crowds the common direction will often just be a mood or a very faint and abstract ideal, something most people will not even be aware of. So the direction or goal works under the surface and much more subtly. In many, if not most areas of their lives the members of first order crowds will behave rationally and independently from the crowd movement they are involved in. Contrary to that, people in second order crowds are usually completely possessed with the goal of the crowd. All other aspects of life move into the background.

In addition to that, as we have seen, there is no critical mass, no discharge in first order crowds and I believe Canetti is right when he says that, without discharge, you cannot actually speak of a veritable crowd. That is why I propose to think of first order crowds as crowds of a lesser degree, and why I like to call them »basic«. Second order crowds undergo a development and are, therefore, if you will »advanced« – they are crowds in the actual sense of the word. Both, however, are crowd phenomena, since they work according to the same mechanisms.

I have considered it necessary to make this distinction because of recent insights in connection with the new science of Socionomics, which shall be our focus in the following. The early scholars of crowd psychology were practically only concerned with second order crowd phenomena. Only Canetti has touched on the realm of first order phenomena when he was talking about slow crowds and the remoteness from the goal that is peculiar to them.[104] But as he was lacking insights that we have today, he did not recognize the altogether different character of that kind of crowd and treated it simply as a special case within second order phenomena. However, for the reasons I have just mentioned, but also for the consequences they imply, I believe it justified to propose a separate category for first order crowd phenomena. Within second order phenomena, the categorizations proposed earlier by scholars can remain.

General crowd characteristics

Let us now look at what it is that makes up a crowd, at what it is that defines it. Just as there have been attempts to categorize crowds, several suggestions have been made as to a list of typical characteristics of crowds. The ones by Gustave Le Bon[105] and Elias Canetti[106], for example, are extremely detailed and accurate, and reflect the huge amount of experience that these two experts had with crowds.

However, as mentioned, crowd experts such as Le Bon or Canetti were particularly concerned with advanced crowds. Because of this, the characteristics that they propose make perfect sense for that category. Yet aspects such as the urge to grow or the love for denseness, which Canetti lists,[107] or impulsiveness and irritability, which Le Bon mentions,[108] do not quite seem to fit for basic crowds or do so only to a limited extent.

For this reason, I will not go into the details of the characteristics listed by Le Bon and Canetti. Instead, in the following I will attempt to come up with a list of those aspects, which seem to me to be a common feature of all crowd phenomena, be they basic or advanced. This means that a lot will be left aside, which the leading figures of crowd psychology considered crucial and which might be deemed indispensable to students of crowd psychology. However, I hope that the distinction between these two kinds of crowds, between basic and advanced crowds, explains why I believe that this is justified.

In my opinion, the following characteristics can be found in all kinds of crowds:

Unity of mind

Key to the understanding of crowds is the unity of mind, which, as stated above, Le Bon called »the law of the mental unity of crowds«. It means that people in crowds are somehow brought into line with respect to a certain idea or mood and, with respect to that, act as individuals only in a limited way. A crowd has its own social reality.[109] This is why a crowd often gives the impression of being an independent organism.

Within crowds, ideas, thoughts and moods can spread extremely fast to infect every individual. Le Bon speaks of »contagion mentale«, mental contagion.[110] This mechanism can be observed regularly in advanced crowds and seems to be operating in basic crowd movements as well.[111] Comparisons have been drawn to epidemics and viruses since studies suggest that crazes and trends of all kinds follow a trajectory similar to an epidemic.[112]

Although it is not at all clear yet how mental contagion works, recent research suggests it might have something to do with the so called mirror cells that can be found in the human brain. These are responsible for our ability to exhibit empathy. Most mirror cells react only to the experience itself, but about 20 % of them, however, fire also at the observation of that experience.[113] Who knows how many of them might fire in a crowd where many people experience the same emotion and the observation of that emotion can be made many times? Although the application of the mirror cell mechanism is still speculation, it might offer an explanation of how ideas and moods spread from brain to brain.

Direction or goal

As Canetti puts it: »The crowd needs a direction. It is in movement and it moves towards a goal. … A crowd exists so long as it has an unattained goal.«[114]

Under section a), unity of mind in terms of ideas, thoughts or moods was mentioned. Those ideas, thoughts or moods constitute the direction in which the crowd moves. They are the goal, the objective that drives the crowd. So whilst unity of mind clearly is the key characteristic, there always needs to be a direction or goal first, which then triggers that unity.

To speak of direction is rather abstract but I believe it is justified, as the goals of a crowd can be very abstract indeed. Especially where basic crowd movements are concerned, it is often a rather abstract ideal that constitutes the crowd's goal. Canetti mentions the example of religious crowds where the goal is far away and can even be something that cannot be reached in this life, such as redemption in the Christian faith.[115] Although this is a very abstract concept, it can be strong enough to form crowds and keep them together over centuries.

In an extreme case, what gives a crowd its direction can even be something that not even a single element of the crowd is aware of. In the basic unconscious crowd movements of our society, it is social mood. This is a topic we will address later on.

Emotion over reason

It is never reason that rules a crowd. The direction or goal is not embraced for a reason that could be logically debated. A crowd is not open for arguments and reasonable discussion.[116] Crowds behave irrationally and emotionally; they behave instinctively. It has been said that man when he becomes part of a crowd falls back to the state of a savage or of a child.[117] In this context Sigmund Freud speaks of collective inhibitions of the mental capacity.[118]

As we shall see more closely later on, it is indeed likely that the source of crowd behavior lies in the primitive sections of our brain, the so-called basal ganglia and the limbic system.[119] These are the sections that are responsible for instinctive and emotional reactions and behavior and they can operate quite independently of the neocortex.

Biological and sociological foundations

Studies suggest that the root of crowd behavior are the primitive portions of the human brain such as the basal ganglia and the limbic system, as has just been mentioned. We share these sections with animals and, indeed, if we look at behavior in the animal kingdom, herd behavior can be observed among countless species. It is, therefore, quite likely for crowd behavior in general to rest on behavioral patterns that developed millions of years ago and that are still active in man today.

We owe such behavioral patterns probably not only to biological foundations but also to evolved rules of conduct. Such rules do not need to be consciously known. Rules in this context can be thought of as »... a propensity or disposition to act or not to act in a certain manner ...«.[120] Just like instincts, rules of conduct are supposed to give an individual and – more importantly – a group of individuals a better chance of survival.[121] Imitation and emulation are such rules. They foster the cohesiveness of a group and thereby make it stronger.

Instinctive herding and flocking serves the same evolutionary goal, namely enhancing the survival of the group or species by providing advantages in different areas such as food supply, mating and protection against predators.[122] Together, evolved and handed-down rules of conduct and instinctive herding behavior are very likely to produce the kind of crowd movements that we can observe among humans today.

Situations of uncertainty[123]

Crowd movements occur when a situation is uncertain and people cannot use reason to decide on how to behave. When there is not enough information in a certain situation or when the overall situation is extremely unstable, people have the tendency to herd and follow what others do.

Whenever we can obtain enough knowledge to form rational conclusions, our neocortex has a good chance of prevailing over the more primitive portions of the brain such as the limbic system. However, if we cannot manage to gather enough data for the neocortex to be able to operate, our limbic system will take over and we will act instinctively and emotionally. And this means that we seek information from others. Whether it is a panic, a football stadium euphoria or a stock market mania, it is always a lack of information that makes people turn to those around them for guidance. It is uncertainty that creates people's other-directedness and induces the propensity to imitate, emulate and herd. We shall hear more about this later on.

Dealing with crowd phenomena

Le Bon says in his book that today, knowledge of crowd psychology is the last resort for a politician who does not want to be controlled by the crowds – controlling them has become too difficult.[124] He said so a hundred years ago and I think it is as true as ever. Crowds cannot be controlled, if this word is meant to express the complete control of every detail. Second order phenomena, in particular, are really beyond control due to their powerful internal dynamics. However, if the word control is meant to suggest the capacity to steer and guide a system, which is how cybernetics understands the term, we find that maybe there actually can be ways of controlling a crowd phenomenon. And, again, the distinction between first and second order crowd phenomena seems useful.

Second order crowds are beyond our capacity to control by anything other than sheer force. It might seem that crowd wizards such as Napoleon or Hitler were able to control them but it appears very doubtful whether they could have redirected the crowds of which they were apparently in control. According to all we know about advanced crowds, it seems much more likely that these seducers, once the internal crowd dynamics had started to operate, simply had no choice but to continue along the way that they had pointed out in the first place. They could create the crowds – one could say that they were catalysts – but they would not have been able to stop them again afterwards. They would have simply got run over because creating a second order crowd phenomenon means unleashing forces that cannot be controlled. Apart from force, there is only one thing that can stop them: time. Just like a chemical reaction, a crowd process will stop as soon as there is no more »material« to fuel it. When the internal dynamics start to falter, the crowd will eventually dissolve.

The key, then, seems to be to prevent second order crowds from coming into being in the first place. This leaves us with first order crowds. We have already seen that within basic crowds the unity of mind is far less developed than in advanced crowds. There are no strong internal dynamics and even the fact that there is a common goal and that the members of a basic crowd are part of a movement is usually not known to them.

Because people are unaware of being part of such a crowd, it seems that it should be possible to either steer or guide or »channel« basic crowd movements in a way that will prevent them from giving birth to advanced crowds or at least to prepare the environment for the outbreak of advanced crowds so that they will only cause minor damage.

This is the main point of concern of this book and in Part IV we shall deal with the question of how this could be done in practice when we look at legislative systems and how they could be changed to tackle this problem. But first, we now have too take a closer look at first order crowd phenomena and this brings us to long waves and the new science of Socionomics.

3.2 Socionomics – the science of social prediction

Socionomics is a new science that deals with human behavioral patterns that enable us to predict the course of society more accurately than ever before. It states a new paradigm, namely that social trends are based on an endogenous human herding tendency manifesting itself in a predictable pattern called the Wave Principle. Following the Wave Principle, social trends are unaffected by outside causes and events and actually constitute their source and engine.

Socionomics was founded by Robert R. Prechter, jun. and first described by him in his book *The Wave Principle of Human Social Behavior and the new Science of Socionomics* in 1999. It is based on work that was conducted by Ralph Nelson Elliott in the stock market in the 1930s. Still rather unknown, Socionomics is gaining momentum among all kinds of scholars who recognize it as a new and valuable tool for the study and better understanding of human behavior. Like all new theories, it has not yet been academically accepted. Indeed, I believe that most professors do not even bother to deal with it. However, I also believe that this is a mistake. Although so far there is not much data available yet with respect to Socionomics, the data that exists and the studies that have been conducted suggest that the key assertions are correct. There is still much work to be done and the shaping of a coherent theory without gaps will still take a long time but it is my conviction that it is no longer justified to ignore this new science. We know enough to work with Socionomics and test it and to include it into our research, which is what I am trying to do here.

I must stress that for the rest of this work I will consider the assumptions and statements of the theory as correct. Of course, I am fully aware of the still rather vague state of it and that any minute something new might be learned which might falsify it. But this is true for any scientific theory. And as already mentioned, I believe that we have enough data supporting the key assertions so we can work with them.

I think the socionomic approach is real progress and can be of tremendous importance and relevance to our understanding and shaping of society. This is why I have decided to include it in this book and indeed base much of it upon it. The following will now introduce Socionomics and its implications.

3.2.1 The Wave Principle

As mentioned above, Socionomics is based on insights that the American accountant Ralph Nelson Elliott gained while studying the stock market in the 1930s. Forced to stay at home in a rocking chair due to anemia, which he barely survived in his sixties, Elliott turned to a meticulous investigation of the history and movements of the Dow Jones Industrial Index. What he found was a pattern that is repetitive in form, but not necessarily in time or amplitude.[125] He called it the »Wave Principle«, described in detail thirteen sub-patterns and explained how they combine to form the Wave Principle.[126] He believed to have found a general principle, a natural law and gave expression to his conviction by naming his major work *Nature's Law,* in which he explained his theory in great detail.

This is not the place to investigate all the details of the Wave pattern. For our purpose a general introduction and overview will be sufficient. If further information is requested I recommend Robert Prechter's book *Elliott Wave Principle,* which he wrote together with A. J. Frost and in which they explain in detail everything there is to know about the Wave Principle.

Fundamentals

The basic pattern

The pattern that Elliott found while studying charts of the Dow Jones is a basic five-wave movement in one direction (motive phase) followed by a counter-movement of three waves in the other direction (corrective phase). Together they form what is called a cycle (Figure 18).[127]

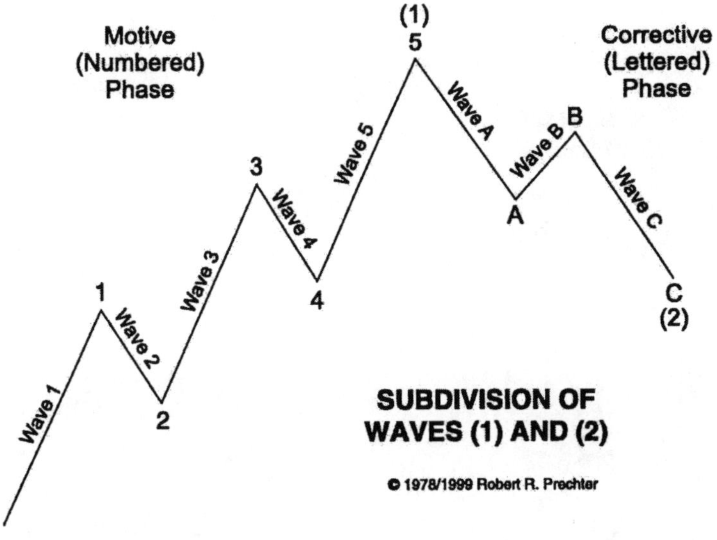

Figure 18: The basic pattern

Source: Prechter, Robert: The Wave Principle of Human Social Behavior and the New Science of Socionomics, 1999

We can see that in the motive phase the directional movement of waves 1, 3 and 5 is interrupted by the counter movement of waves 2 and 4 just as wave B interrupts the movement of waves A and C in the corrective phase. It looks as if these interruptions were necessary so that overall directional movement can happen at all. We shall have a look at the possible reason for this a little later.

Recursion

We already got to know the principle of recursion when we introduced the Viable System Model of Stafford Beer in the past chapter. The reader may recall that every viable system consists of and is part of another viable system.

The Wave Principle functions in a similar manner. A Cycle such as in Figure 18 constitutes the first two waves of the motive phase of a cycle of the next higher level of recursion.[128] At the same time waves (1) and (2) of the cycle are a cycle themselves on the next lower level of recursion and look the same as the cycle in Figure 18. The Wave pattern therefore combines to form higher and higher levels of recursion with the same shape. Figures 19 and 20 show what is meant by this.

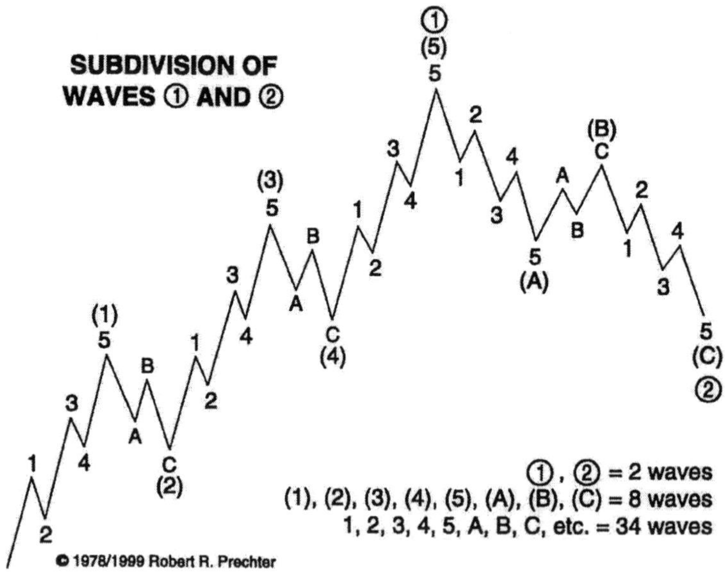

Figure 19: Two levels of recursion

Source: Prechter, Robert: The Wave Principle of Human Social Behavior and the New Science of Socionomics, 1999

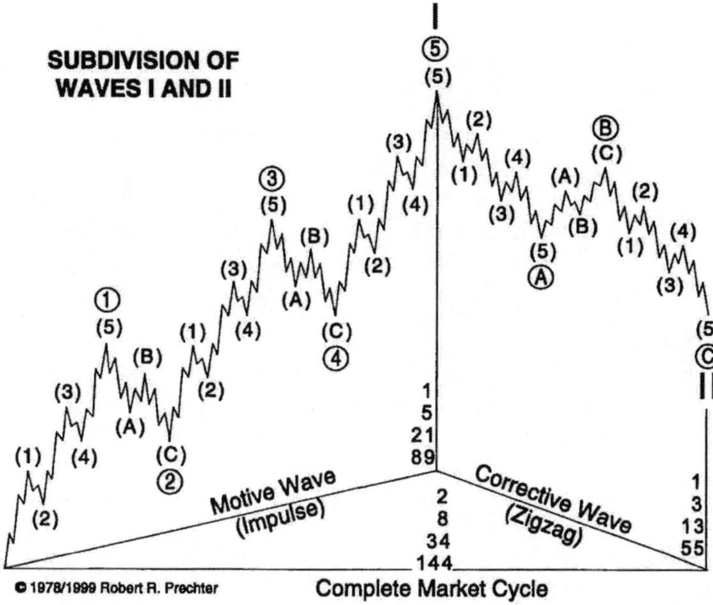

Figure 20: Three levels of recursion

Source: Prechter, Robert: The Wave Principle of Human Social Behavior and the New Science of Socionomics, 1999

It should be apparent that the pattern depicts self-similarity just as does Beer's Viable System Model. And just as the VSM this self-similarity is restricted to the structure, the form, the pattern. The specific details of the Viable System can vary greatly and, as mentioned above, time and amplitude of the Wave Principle are also variable. What remains constant despite this is the form.[129]

One more thing needs to be added, which becomes apparent in Figures 19 and 20. Motive waves do not always point upwards just as corrective waves do not always point downwards. Whether a phase is called motive or corrective does not depend on the absolute direction but on the relative direction, i. e. on the direction of the wave of the next higher level of recursion.[130] In Figure 20, wave Ⓐ consists of five waves because the overall movement of wave II is down and therefore wave Ⓐ is a motive wave.

Why 5–3?

There seem to be two reasons why a 5–3 pattern might be a logical consequence[131]: Firstly, progress can only happen where there is fluctuation. And »progress must include setbacks and net change over time«. Secondly, a 5–3 pattern is the minimum that is required in a movement that includes fluctuation and progress, when the only constraint is that odd-numbered waves are longer than even-numbered ones. So 5–3 is necessary but also sufficient – another parallel to the VSM. A 3–1 movement would not allow for fluctuation in the corrective phase. And even-numbered cycles would mean no progress at all.

We shall see later that the Wave Principle appears to have a natural basis and that 5–3 combinations can be found in many areas where there needs to be fluctuation and progress. »Nature typically follows the most efficient path«.[132]

Fractal structure

Self-similarity is something that we commonly find in nature in structures that we have come to call fractal. Fractals are objects that are nonlinear and self-similar in that a part of a fractal looks similar to the whole.

Fractal geometry distinguishes between two kinds of fractals:

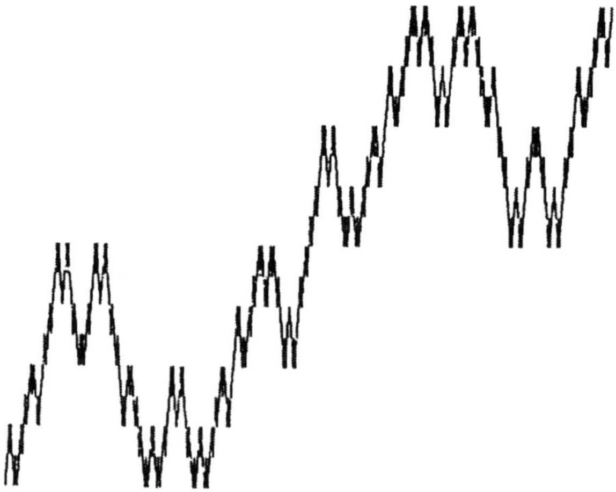

Figure 21: A self-identical fractal

Source: Prechter, Robert: The Wave Principle of Human Social Behavior and the New Science of Socionomics, 1999

Self-identical fractals

A self-identical fractal is an object whose parts are identical with the whole.[133] This means that no matter what level of recursion you are looking at it looks exactly the same as the highest level of recursion being in this case the whole object. Figure 21 depicts such a fractal.

Indefinite fractals

The only way in which indefinite fractals depict self-similarity is that there is no similarity between the different levels of recursion.[134] Every level is equally irregular. A typical example of an indefinite fractal is a coastline. A given part of the coastline gives no hint as to whether that part is 200 meters or 200 kilometers in length. Without being given the scale there is no clue as to the distance from which you are looking at it. A coastline is similarly irregular at all scales.

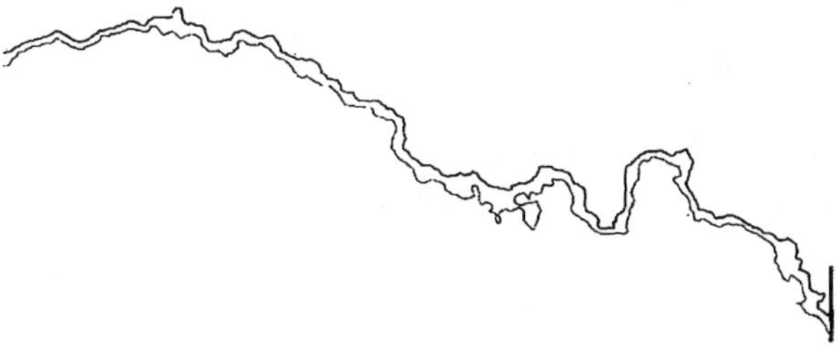

Figure 22: A coast line – an indefinite fractal

Source: Prechter, Robert: The Wave Principle of Human Social Behavior and the New Science of Socionomics, 1999

Robust fractals

Prechter suggests introducing a third type of fractal, which he calls robust. The Elliott Wave pattern clearly shows self-similarity to a high degree but neither are the different levels of recursion identical nor are they completely irregular. As we have seen the pattern is formological, i. e. the overall form remains the same but the way in which the pattern can unfold is highly variable. So the Wave pattern seems to be something between the two classical categories. It is a fractal of intermediate specificity.[135]

Prechter suggests the term robust fractal because, as we shall see shortly, nature seems to employ this kind of intermediate fractal whenever a structure needs to be robust, i. e. resistant to changes in its environment. Resistance of this kind requires flexibility and adaptability within a given structure and robust fractals seem to be able to provide just that.

Fibonacci mathematics

It has been said that the form of the Wave pattern remains constant and that only its specific appearance such as amplitude or the period of time over which it develops changes. This does not mean, however, that the development of these varying attributes is random. It follows a particular kind of mathematics that can also be found in the pattern itself. This specific kind of mathematics is called Fibonacci mathematics.

THE FIBONACCI SEQUENCE

Leonardo Fibonacci, also called Leonardo of Pisa (ca. 1170 – ca. 1240), is considered the first great mathematician of the occident. He was the son of a diplomat and although born in Pisa, he grew up in North Africa due to his father's work. In his younger years, he was able to travel extensively in the Arabic world and thereby got in touch with Arabic mathematics. At around 1200 A. D. he returned to Pisa where he published his book *liber abaci,* still famous today. Among other things, it introduced Arabic figures and the figure 0 to the occident where they had been unknown until then. Moreover, in his book Fibonacci described the so-called Fibonacci sequence, now named after him, which is:

1, 1, 2, 3, 5, 8, 13, 21, 34, 55, 89, 144, …

Looking at the sequence we again encounter recursion. The sum of two successive figures equals the next figure in the sequence. 1 + 1 = 2, 1+ 2 = 3, 2 + 3 = 5, and so on. Therefore, the sequence can also be written in a general recursive formula:

$fn = fn_{-1} + fn_{-2}$
$f_0 = 0$
$f_1 = 1$

THE GOLDEN RATIO

Except for the recursive feature of the Fibonacci sequence, we can observe another peculiarity that concerns its ratio. If we divide two successive numbers in the sequence, we find that the result is approximately 0.618 or 1.618 depending on whether we divide the lower number by the higher or the other way around. For the first few numbers the deviation is rather large, but the higher the numbers get the more accurate the ratio approaches 0.618 or, more accurately, 0.618034… This number is the irrational number Phi.

Phi seems to play an important part in nature and has, at all times, fascinated people because of its aesthetic component: It can be found in the architecture of the ancient Egyptians and Greeks and in the buildings of the Renaissance such as Notre Dame cathedral. And modern buildings such as the CN Tower in Toronto or the UN building in New York City contain Phi as well. In art, the Golden Ratio or Golden Section can be found in paintings by Leonardo da Vinci and Salvador Dali, and George Pierre Seurat is said to have »attacked every canvas by the golden section«. We can find Phi in music and acoustics, in design and many other areas of our lives.[136] In short, Phi is ubiquitous.

Fibonacci in the Wave Principle

The first to notice that the Fibonacci sequence could be important for the Wave Principle was not Elliott himself. Charles Collins, then Elliott's pub-

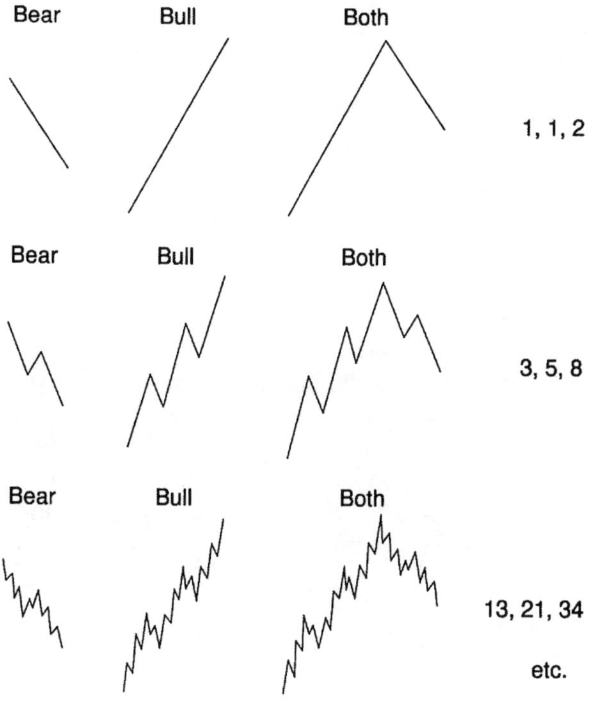

Figure 23: Fibonacci in the Wave Principle

Source: Prechter, Robert: The Wave Principle of Human Social Behavior and the New Science of Socionomics, 1999

lisher and a well-known investment adviser, was the first to see the connection and told Elliott, who then conducted some research on the issue. His conclusions were then published in his major work Nature's Law in 1940.[137]

Figure 23 makes clear how the Wave Pattern and the Fibonacci sequence are connected. The number of waves in each cycle and in each phase of a cycle corresponds with a Fibonacci number.

The recursion both in the Wave Principle and in the Fibonacci sequence can well be seen in Figure 24, which depicts a logarithmic Fibonacci spiral in combination with an idealized form of the Wave Principle.

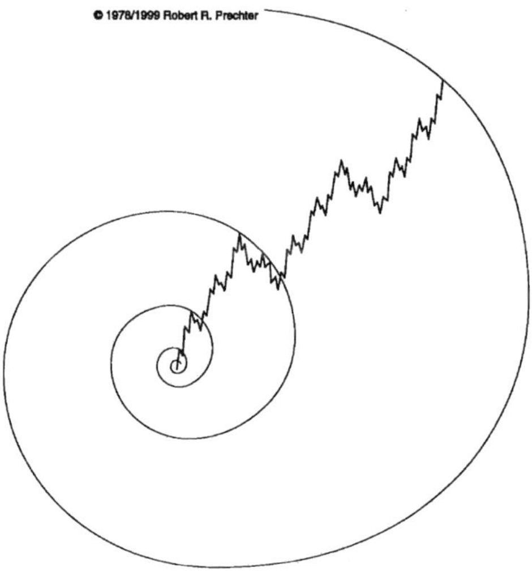

Figure 24: The Wave Principle in a Fibonacci spiral

Source: Prechter, Robert: The Wave Principle of Human Social Behavior and the New Science of Socionomics, 1999

Moreover, the Fibonacci ratio, which is Phi, can be observed in several price relationships among waves in the Wave Principle. In ratio analysis, Phi is also used to investigate the relationship in time and amplitude of one wave to another.

Robust fractals and Fibonacci in nature and the human body

It was stated at the very beginning of this chapter that the Wave Principle is based on endogenous human herding behavior. Before we turn to the biological, sociological and psychological foundations to see what the source of this herding behavior, and therefore of the Wave Principle, could be it might be useful to have a look at robust fractal forms and Fibonacci mathematics in nature and in our own body. Having realized to what extent these structures and properties suffuse nature and even our very selves might make it easier to understand and accept that there could well be a link between the stock market, biological and sociological basic human functions and the patterned trends of human social behavior in general, as Robert Prechter argues.

Robust fractals, spirals and Fibonacci numbers can be observed separately but they occur just as often together. It seems that nature uses these tools whenever self-organizing systems need to grow and prosper and therefore exhibit robustness towards external forces and efficiency.[138]

These universal forms can be found in living and non-living things, in the smallest forms such as atoms and in the largest such as galaxies. They play a role in plant life and dominate the relationship of our body parts to one another. They can even be found in our sensory organs and our brain.

Robust fractals and spirals

We have already seen how the Wave Principle reflects fractal and spiral structure as well as waves. Prechter calls them universal forms and speaks of their ubiquity in nature because they can be found not only in the stock market but throughout nature in various forms and shapes. He speculates that robust fractals as well as spirals are actually phenomena of the same kind. Nature seems to use these structures whenever growth over time is involved that needs to show robustness, flexibility and adaptability to outside influences.

Waves

The unfolding of the waves of the movements of the stock market has already been explained above and we could see how it reflects robust fractal structure, as the overall form remains constant on all levels of recursion whilst time and amplitude are variable. The same seems to hold true for the human heartbeat as studies suggest. Researchers from Boston University and Harvard Medical School report to have found the following:

»Plotting the time intervals [between beats] on a graph creates an interesting pattern. It's a complex, jagged line looking a little like a mountain range. The nature of the jagged pattern looks the same when it's graphed for a short time period – say minutes – or over a longer time, like 24 hours, corresponding to thousands of heartbeats. This similar structure persisting over different scales is what mathematicians call a fractal.«[139]

And researchers at MIT, Harvard Medical School and Boston University found a fractal wave pattern in the human nucleotide sequence.

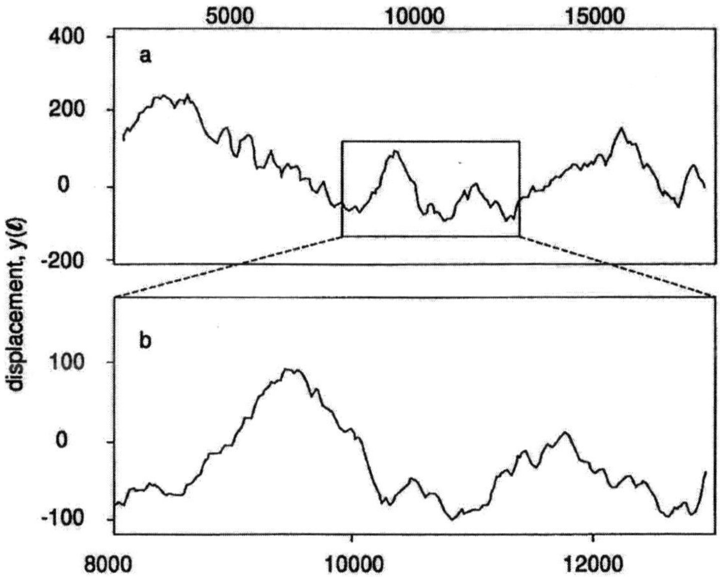

Figure 25: A fractal pattern in the human nucleotide sequence
Source: Prechter, Robert: The Wave Principle of Human Social Behavior and the New Science of Socionomics, 1999

Branching fractals
Another model example for robust fractal growth are branching fractals. Prechter likes to refer to this kind of growth as arboration.[140] He derives the expression from the Latin word for tree, arbor, due to the tree-like shape of things that display arboration.

Arbora, i. e. branching fractals can be found in many places. As the word suggests, trees are certainly branching fractals, but so are many plants of all sizes. Human and animal extremities are arbora. Our blood vessels continue to branch down to the tiniest capillaries and our bronchial system branches just like it. It is even called a bronchial tree. We find branching structures in our intestines and in our nervous system the nerve cells are arbora. Even our brain is an arborum.[141]

Figure 26: A tree is a branching fractal
Source: © Bernad – Fotolia.com

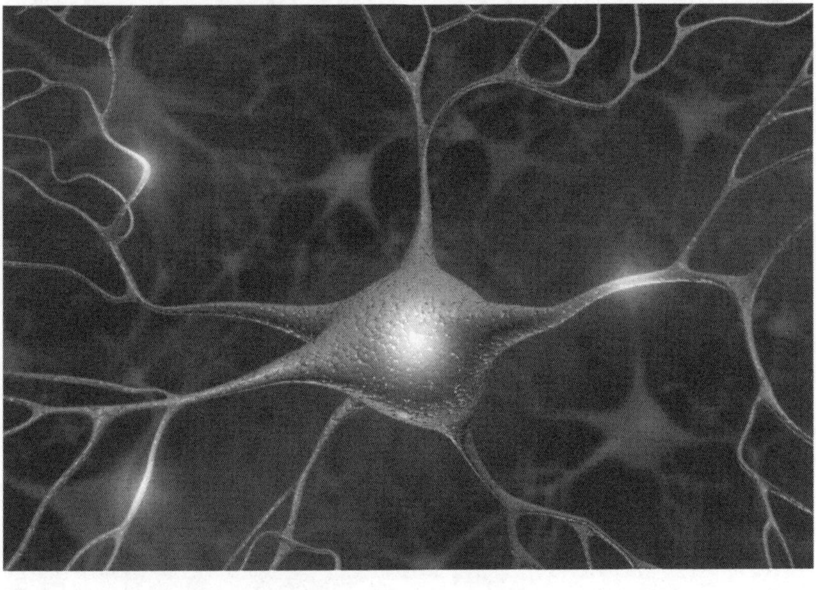

Figure 27: Human nerve cell
Source: © ktsdesign – Fotolia.com

There are branching fractal structures in non-living things as well. A bolt of lightning is a branching fractal as is a river system with a delta. And chemical diffusions often take the shape of an arborum.

Figure 28: A branching river system
Source: http://veimages.gsfc.nasa.gov/3451/landsat_art_lena_lrg.jpg.

Prechter suggests that even family trees could be interpreted as branching fractals.[142] This would in a way imply that evolution itself might work by means of robust fractal structures.

Spirals

Just as waves and branching fractals are ubiquitous forms found in the world all around us, so are spirals. Nature seems to be using spiral structures, although they are identical fractals, for much the same purpose as it uses robust fractals.[143] They appear to be important for »growing systems that involve bipolarity, stress and fluctuation«.[144] Many animals and plants exhibit spiral growth. And so does our body, for instance in our sensory organs.

Figure 29: Nautilus
Source: © bluemap – Fotolia.com

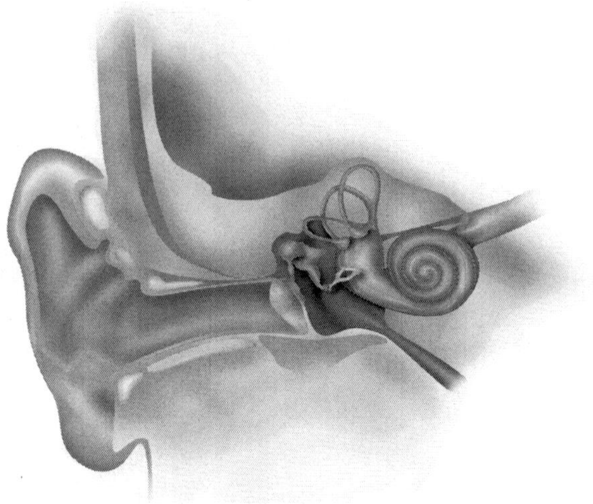

Figure 30: Spiral cochlea in the ear
Source: © ingenium-design.de – Fotolia.com

In non-living nature we can find spirals e. g. in waves, tropical storms, whirlpools or galaxies. And even atomic particles move in spirals as they bounce back off the surface of an obstacle.

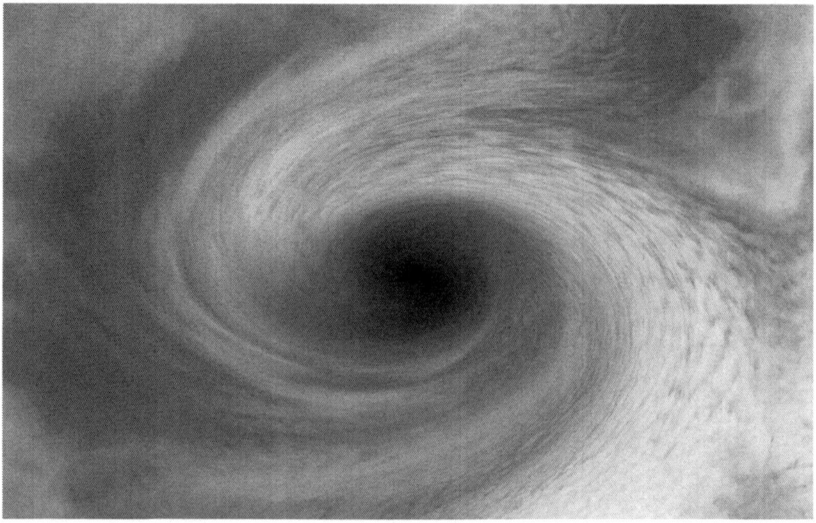

Figure 31: Hurricane
Source: © Peter Kirschner – Fotolia.com

Figure 32: Spiral galaxy
Source: http://www.spacetelescope.org/images/html/opo0501a.html

Fractals, especially robust fractals and spirals, are ever-present in non-living nature, in plant, animal and human life. »Waves and arbora become more complex and spirals more expanded, as time proceeds«.[145] This is not the case with static structures such as crystals or magnets. »The difference appears to be that static fractals are phenomena of space, while robust fractals are growth patterns through time«.[146] Wherever growth is involved, we can often find robust fractals or spirals. They seem to be essential for progress and it looks as if this also holds true for the progress of human society.

THE FIBONACCI SEQUENCE

Just like robust fractals and spirals, the Fibonacci sequence and ratio can often be found when growth and growing, self-organizing systems are involved. Many plants branch to produce the Fibonacci sequence, as do certain chemical diffusions as studies show.[147] The number of seeds in the blossoms of many flowers follows the Fibonacci sequence and seashells (see Figure 29) spiral according to Fibonacci mathematics.

Moreover, the Fibonacci ratio occurs throughout our entire body. Our body parts are related to each other by Phi ratios just like our face is dominated by it. Certain microtubules in the brain possess a Fibonacci number of cells[148], the nucleotide spirals of our DNA show properties that are close to Phi, and the spiral cochlea of the ear (see Figure 30) is a Fibonacci spiral.[149] There is even evidence that the electronic impulses in the neurons of our brain are governed by a ratio that is very close to Phi. »... that the peak negative charge of the cells in each neuron is 70/110, or .636, and the peak positive charge is 40/110, or .364, of the entire range of its charge. These ratios are very close to the Fibonacci ratios, .618 and .382«.[150]

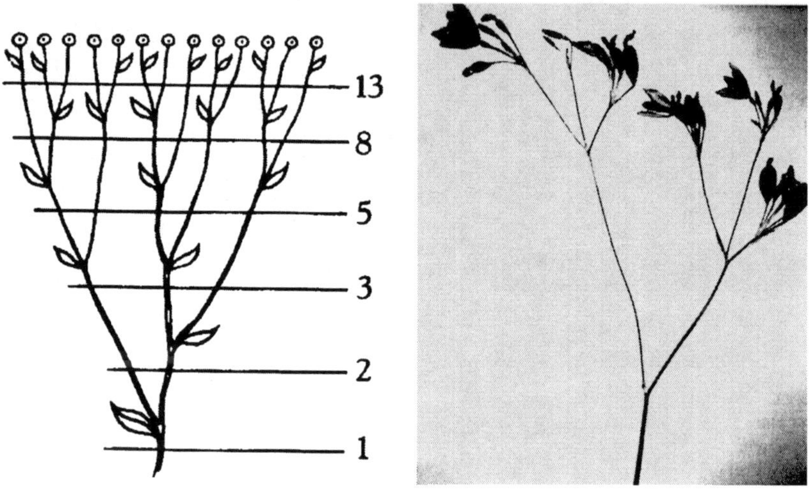

Figure 33: Fibonacci in branching plants

Source: Prechter, Robert: The Wave Principle of Human Social Behavior and the New Science of Socionomics, 1999

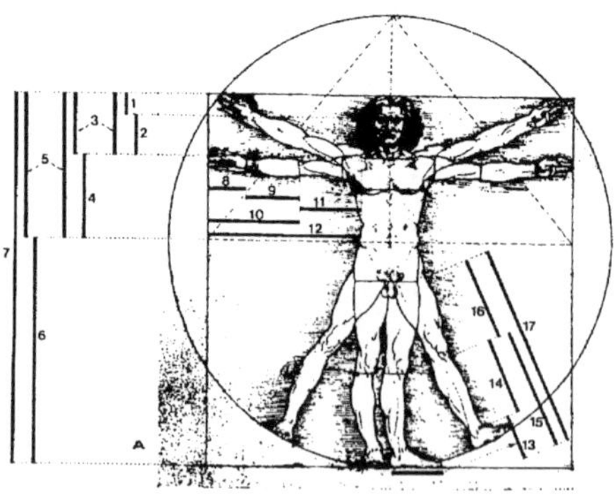

1 : 2 = 2 : 3 = 3 : 4 = 4 : 5 = 6 : 7 = 8 : 9 =9 : 10 =
10 : 12 = 11: 10 = 13 :14 = 14 : 15 = 16: 15 = 15 : 17 = 0.618±

Figure 34: Phi in the human body according to Leonardo da Vinci

Source: © HP_Photo– Fotolia.com

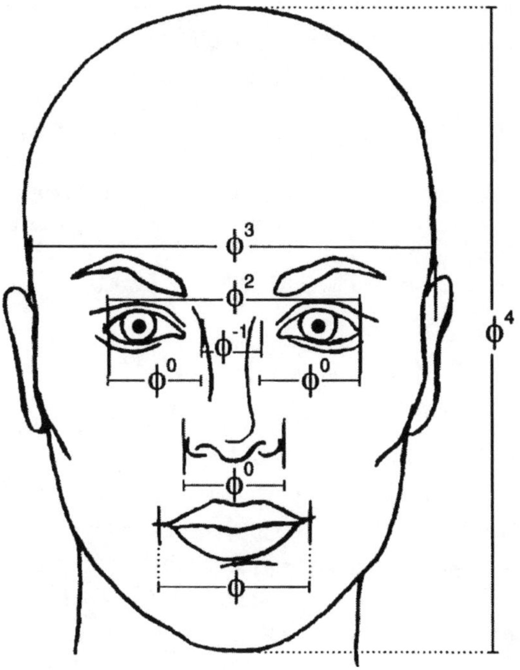

Figure 35: Phi in the human face

Source: Prechter, Robert: The Wave Principle of Human Social Behavior and the New Science of Socionomics, 1999

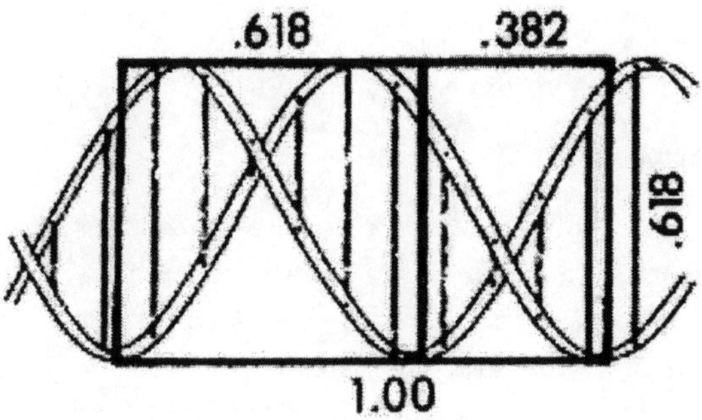

Figure 36: Phi in the human DNA

Source: Prechter, Robert: The Wave Principle of Human Social Behavior and the New Science of Socionomics, 1999

There are theories suggesting that indeed the reason why we think of the Golden Ratio as aesthetic and find things beautiful that are governed by it, is that our sensory organs and even our brain are governed by it as well.

»Aesthetic feeling is the product of the complexity of an object and the degree of match of that object with the logarithmic spiral form in the brain. If this conclusion is true, it might explain why so many studies show that people consistently demonstrate a preference for Fibonacci proportions in objects and why so many artists throughout history, from ancient Egyptian and Greek architects to Leonardo da Vinci, have held a special fascination for Fibonacci relationships consciously including them in their creations«.[151]

Conclusions

Since science has only just started to look more closely at nature and the human body from the point of view of fractals and Fibonacci, we do not have enough data yet to tell to what extent these structures govern our world and ourselves. It seems clear, however, that they play an extremely important role for growth processes and the development of self-organizing systems. Fractals appear to be »tools of efficiency, efficacy and robustness«.[152] Fibonacci seems to play a role when growth involves »bipolarity, stress and fluctuation«.[153]

We shall now turn to the biological and sociological sources of the Wave Principle. The goal will be to show how the human brain, which is based on fractal and Fibonacci processes, is responsible for us behaving in a way that creates exactly the same kind of pattern in our social actions as can be found in the very structures of which we are made up.

The foundation of the Wave Principle in Biology, Sociology and Psychology[154]

Unconscious herding behavior

According to Prechter, the source of the Wave Principle is an unconscious endogenous herding impulse, i. e. unconscious crowd behavior, which brings people into line and creates, in the aggregate, the Wave Principle as the pattern of human social behavior. Prechter bases this assumption on the theory of Paul MacLean, the former head of the Laboratory for Brain Evolution at the National Institute of Mental Health in the United States.

MacLean's theory presents evidence which supports the concept of a »triune« brain. According to MacLean, there are basically three parts of the brain that can be distinguished, the basal ganglia, the limbic system and the neocortex, which all correspond to particular phases of evolution in our development.[155] Some important observations made by MacLean with respect to this are the following:

1. Our brain stem is similar to the brain of reptiles. Mammals in general have the brain stem and in addition to it a limbic system. It is not until the development of primates that a significant neocortex can be observed.
2. The placement of these three brain parts is like a box of building blocks. They are piled up on each other from the inside to the outside and bottom to top.
3. During the development of the human fetus in the womb, the three parts grow according to their evolutionary history. First there are the basal ganglia. From them grows the limbic system and lastly the neocortex in turn develops from cells of the limbic system.
4. In children, the three brain sections also »mature« in the same order described above.
5. Clinical tests suggest that indeed each portion of the brain is responsible for functions and behavior that relate to the animal ancestors in whom they are dominant.

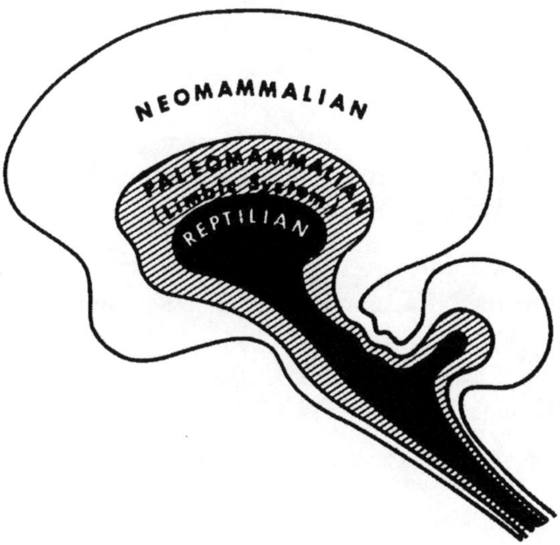

Figure 37: The triune brain

Source: Prechter, Robert: The Wave Principle of Human Social Behavior and the New Science of Socionomics, 1999

These aspects of a still traceable evolutionary path of our brain development are important because the connection to evolution »explains why man has a mind that includes unconscious, impulsive mentation«.[156]

To understand this »unconscious, impulsive mentation«, it is important to know what functions the three sections of the brain perform[157]:

Basal ganglia: The basal ganglia are responsible for behavior, which we call instinctive. This includes for example mating behavior, migration, fleeing, fighting, territorialism, the reaction to fear and also herding, schooling and flocking, which is especially important from our point of view in this book.

Limbic system: The limbic system, which developed next, is the place where our emotions reside. It actually intensifies the instincts of the basal ganglia and thereby strengthens primitive life-preserving behavior. »The limbic system underlies the subjective experience of ... emotional feelings that guide behavior required for self-preservation and the preservation of the species.«[158]

Neocortex: The neocortex, then, is where our reasoning and logical thinking take place.

The interesting thing is that the two primitive portions of the brain, i. e. the basal ganglia and the limbic system, can work quite independently from and also faster than our neocortex. Research conducted at the Laboratory of Neurobiology at Cornell Medical Center has shown that »emotion and corresponding reaction can occur both independently of and prior to thought«.[159]

In general, there are four advantages that the limbic system holds over the neocortex and that allow the former in certain situations to retain the upper hand over the latter[160]:

1. The limbic system is faster than the neocortex.
2. The limbic system itself regulates the amplitude of the emotions it sends out.
3. It has no concept of time. »Whatever it wants, it wants now«[161].
4. Feelings of reality and personal identity are located in the limbic system. This is why our emotions are so important to us and why we often react in an unreasonably fierce manner when they are challenged »even if that challenge comes from reality itself«[162].

As actions triggered by the basal ganglia and the limbic system are responses that developed many hundreds of millions of years ago and as they are unconscious, MacLean in his theory of the triune brain speaks of paleomentation to distinguish this kind of thinking from rational thought. He uses the term to »denote impulsive thought patterns derived from the primitive portions of the brain«.[163]

Having seen what the relationship between our ancient brain parts and the neocortex is and how the limbic system can, at times, dominate over our reasoning, we now need to come back to man's herding tendency. As we have seen above, it, too, is triggered by the basal ganglia and supported by the limbic system. The trend to herd and thereby belong to a group seems to have been an evolutionary advantage in the struggle for survival for many animal species[164]:

1. It improves activities that are necessary for survival, such as the search for food or a mate.
2. In a group the chance of survival when attacked by a predator increases.
3. The chance of being killed by members of the same group because of perceived strangeness is greatly reduced.

The last point may appear odd but there are studies suggesting that »sameness« within a group is an advantage to the survival of the species. It increases the cohesion of the group and thereby makes it stronger. In the early stages of human development, rules of conduct might have served just this purpose. Imitation and behavior according to the rules of a group strengthen the group and are positive for the prevalence of this group over another.[165]

A very important point is that man's unconscious herding behavior kicks in only in particular situations. We saw in the last chapter that a common characteristic of crowd phenomena is that they always occur in situations of uncertainty, i.e. in situations that lack knowledge and information about how people should behave. This is exactly the sort of situation that the limbic system needs to prevail over the neocortex. Our cerebrum needs facts and information to make reasonable decisions. In case such input is missing, reactions take over that go back to earlier evolutionary phases of development – the limbic system assumes control.

»As a primitive tool of survival, emotional impulses from the limbic system impel a desire among individuals to seek signals from others in matters of knowledge and behavior and therefore to align their feelings and convictions with those of the group. … Dependence most easily substitutes for rigorous reasoning when knowledge is lacking or logic irrelevant.«[166]

This psychological interdependence[167] can easily be observed in financial markets. There, the large majority of people who put their money into such markets do not have sufficient knowledge and information to decide what the right decision to make really is. In Prechter's words:

»Outwardly, they [investors] appear rational. Inside, their unconscious is in control. They are driven to follow the herd because they do not have firsthand knowledge adequate to form an independent conviction… The unconscious says: You have little basis upon which to exercise reason; your only alternative is to assume that the herd knows where it's going.«[168]

This clearly reflects people's other-directedness. There are also studies suggesting that this is true even for professional analysts. »The more analysts are wrong, … the more their herding behavior increases and the less accurate their estimates get.«[169]

Herd behavior is a primitive instinct that has survived in man over millions of years. It has proved to be an efficient evolutionary tool in the competition for survival among countless animals and even among humans. Turning to others for information is, no doubt, useful in many situations. But today, there are also situations when herding can be harmful. Not always is »going with the flow« the best alternative.

»In a great number of situations, hoping and herding can contribute to your well-being. Not in financial markets. In many cases, panicking and fleeing when others do cuts your risk. Not in financial markets. Paradoxically, then, it is not a confirmation of your correct posture when you look around and can comfortably say, ›Everybody out there agrees with me‹. It is a warning.«[170]

Imitation and handed-down rules of conduct

It has briefly been mentioned that imitation and handed-down rules might account for a good part of human behavior. Research with animals, especially insects that show swarm behavior, suggests that rule following already plays an important role at the early stages of evolution. In their article Swarm Intelligence: A Whole New Way to Think About Business, Eric Bonabeau and Christopher Meyer claim the following: »Perhaps the most powerful – and fascinating – insight from swarm intelligence is that complex collective behavior can emerge from individuals following simple rules.«[171]

Such behavioral patterns based on rule following serve the same sort of purpose as the instincts that make us herd and flock: They increase the chances of survival of individuals and groups. And just as our instincts are unconscious so are these rules of conduct.

»They have thus not developed as the recognized conditions for the achievement of a known purpose, but have evolved because the groups who practiced them were more successful and displaced others. They were rules which, given the kind of environment in which man lived, secured that a greater number of the groups or individuals practicing them would survive«.[172]

Now, it seems difficult to tell the exact difference between instincts and rules. After all, it could be argued that instincts, which make us obey a particular behavioral pattern, are rules as well. The difference could be that instincts are genetically encoded, whereas rules are mentally encoded. We could thus speak of genetically encoded rules and social rules. Social rules could, therefore, be viewed as cultural products, which evolved in later phases of human evolution.

»The differences between the rules … has led to a super-imposition of not merely three layers of rules, but of many more, according as traditions have been preserved from the successive stages through which cultural evolution has passed. The consequence is that modern man is torn by conflicts, which torment him and force him into ever-accelerating further changes. There is, of course, in the first instance, the solid, i. e. little changing foundation of genetically inherited, 'instinctive' drives which are determined by his physiological structure. There are then all the remains of the traditions acquired in the successive types of social structures through which he has passed – rules which he did not deliberately choose but which have spread because some practices enhanced the prosperity of certain groups and led to their expansion…«[173]

Our traditionally handed-down rules of conduct and our instincts exist next to each other and it seems very probable that not the one or the other is responsible for man's crowd behavior but that both work together to create his unconscious herding tendency.

Mentational propensities

Human unconscious herding behavior seems to be the driving force behind the Wave Principle. But this cannot be all that there is to it. Herding alone would not explain why with the Wave Principle there is a distinct and to some extent predictable pattern in human social behavior. There needs to be another aspect to fill the gap.

Several studies support the assumption that this missing link could be certain particular tendencies in people's mentational behavior when making decisions. In this behavior, the Fibonacci ratio plays a key role. Already in 1955, G. A. Kelly suggested that people use bipolar constructs when judging and assessing the world around them. He proposed that every person judges, for example, others on a scale between a positive and a negative pole. The interesting thing is that experiments have shown that the average judgment in value-neutral situations is not 0.50 but actually 0.62 toward the positive end of the scale.[174] The reader will remember that 0.62 is the Fibonacci ratio Phi.

A lot of research was conducted on this matter by the two psychologists Vladimir Lefebvre at the University of California at Irvine and Jack Adams-Webber of Brook University. They conducted several experiments on people's decision-making behavior in value-neutral situations and their findings support the assumption that Phi plays a central role. Whenever they asked subjects to make a choice between two options about which they felt rather neutral and/or did not possess much knowledge, the results divided in a ratio of 62 % to 38 % on the average. The same happened when people who had to evaluate acquaintances and friends in terms of a positive and a negative pole picked the positive pole by 62 % on average. And in an experiment where people were asked to judge the »lightness« of gray paper compared to that of solid white and solid black, most of them marked it either 62 % or 38 % light.[175]

When making decisions in value-neutral situations or under circumstances that do not offer enough knowledge and information, i. e. in situations of uncertainty, people avoid making balanced decisions. »When people say they feel 50/50 on a subject, chances are it's more like 62/38.«[176] And this ratio always tends towards the option about which people are positively biased.

People tend to make choices that are 61.8 % optimistic and 38.2 % pessimistic on the average. This clearly does not mean that everybody behaves like this. As people differ extremely so does their behavior in such situations as described above. Not all people are subject to their unconscious to the same degree. But given a large number of people, human behavior tends towards the Fibonacci ratio. »Phi is what the mind starts with.«[177]

Conclusions – a synthesis

We have seen that man's unconscious herding behavior as well as his tendency towards Phi-biased decisions occur in situations of uncertainty. Both of them are therefore triggered by the limbic system for it is this the part of the brain that controls our thinking and acting when there is not enough information upon which to base our decisions. At the same time we have seen how fractal structures, Fibonacci numbers and the Fibonacci ratio Phi suffuse nature and indeed even our entire body. It has been suggested that even our brain is a robust branching fractal and that neurons operate in relationships astonishingly close to Phi. Now, could it be that because of this fractal and Fibonacci-based functioning of our limbic system our thinking, our actions and our behavior follow the same pattern when we are in situations in which the limbic system rules? And to go one step further: When people interact in a world which is all too often characterized by a lack of information and knowledge and which in many parts of their lives leaves them with »gut decisions« which are controlled by the limbic system, could it not be that people's behavior on the aggregate follows this pattern as well? We have discussed this pattern in detail: It is the Wave Principle. What it reflects is aggregate social mood.

3.2.2 Socionomics

Social mood

R. N. Elliott once said that »human emotions ... are rhythmical« and that their waves dominate »all human activities, whether it is business, politics, or the pursuit of pleasure.«[178] This reveals that Elliott already assumed that the pattern which he had found in the stock market is actually a general principle of human social behavior and that the moves of the financial markets are but one manifestation of this principle. He never said so clearly, though, and for decades after him the Wave Principle was only applied in the stock market arena.

It was Robert Prechter who in the second half of the 1980s took the theory of the Wave Principle one step further in his papers »Popular Culture and the Stock Market« and »The Fractal Design of Social Progress« and thereby started to apply it to social phenomena in general. His assumption is the same as Elliott's, but he states it in a loud and clear way: »The Wave Principle is to sociology and related sciences what Newton's laws were to physics«.[179]

In the previous chapter we got to know the Wave Principle in detail, saw how its structural features can be found as general principles in nature and the human body, and had a look at its possible biological, sociological and psychological foundations. It was then suggested that what can be found in the individuals' biological and behavioral pattern could also lead to the manifestation of this pattern in man's social behavior overall. The Wave

Principle as it can be found in the stock market, should, therefore, be just one obvious manifestation and it should be possible to find it in all human social trends.

However, before we have a closer look at whether this indeed is so we need to introduce the term social mood. Social mood could maybe be described as the aggregate, unconscious, impulsive affective state in which a particular social environment is at a given moment. Triggered and governed by the limbic system, this state is variable in that it is reflected by and follows the Wave Principle.

Still, social mood is a rather vague term. It cannot be discerned clearly, but becomes manifest in the different kinds of feelings and outbursts that can be observed regularly in our world: On an individual level, it is someone deciding to go see a box fight instead of a basketball game. On a societal level, it would be people demonstrating for world peace or youths setting cars and buildings on fire and battling the police.

There indeed »appears to be a social polarity that underlies all social interaction.«[180] As mood is positive or negative, we can distinguish between positive and negative poles or extremes of social mood. Depending on where in the Wave pattern society is, we can therefore observe either a net positive mood or a net negative mood.

However, to know what we are really talking about, social mood needs to be broken down to the specific feelings that come with it. Prechter recognizes the following bipolar manifestations of mood[181]:

Positive mood	**Negative mood**
adventurousness	protectionism
benevolence	malevolence
clarity	fuzziness
concord	discord
confidence	fear
constructiveness	destructiveness
daring	defensiveness
ebullience	depression
inclusion	exclusion
liberality	restriction
optimism	pessimism
supportiveness	opposition
togetherness	separatism

Knowing what kind of feelings one has to expect makes the concept of social mood a bit clearer. But what we see in the news and in everyday life is usually not the mood itself but concrete actions and events that result from it. Therefore, it is important to link actions and events to social mood in order to get a clear picture. Prechter gives the following examples[182]:

1. *Inclusion/Exclusion:* A rising mood leads to feelings of social brotherhood and acceptance among races, religions and political territories, as well as toward animals, plants and proposed aliens. A falling mood leads to apartheid, religious animosity, cavalier cruelty, secession, independence movements and images of aliens as monsters.
2. *Confidence/Fear:* A rising mood leads to speculation in the stock market and in business. A falling mood causes risk aversion in the stock market and business.
3. *Concord/Discord:* A rising mood leads to a substantial consensus in politics, culture and social vision; a falling mood leads to a divided, radical climate. After the social mood has risen for a number of years, the society tends to be peaceful; after it has fallen for a number of years, it tends to become involved in wars.

Mood manifestations vary in intensity. Accordingly, the effect that social mood has on society varies as well. As the Wave Principle is recursive, the effects that a trend will have depend on the level of recursion on which a trend occurs. The higher the level of recursion is, the more intense the mood manifestations will be and the more extreme the events and actions which make the headlines of the news.

What has been said so far refers to the overall social mood on the aggregate, i. e. the mood that dominates society as a whole. However, there are of course trends and microsystems that are much smaller than that. »Each city, state, political movement, religion and sport has its own waves.«[183] They, too, reflect the Wave Principle but on a much narrower scale. So smaller trends are part of larger ones, and microsystems are part of macrosystems. What we got to know in the Viable System Model is true for »wave-systems« as well. Each one is part of and consists of another one. Some of these smaller aggregations will reflect the overall trend, but others might not. For a socionomist it is therefore important to »obtain as much data as possible to isolate each phenomenon he studies, as each one has its own wave structure. … Together, all the waves of all the aggregations weave the fabric of social life.«[184]

Social trends

We have seen that the moves of the stock market follow the Wave Principle. Now, if it is true that social mood in general follows the Wave Principle as well, there would have to be a correlation between the ups and downs of the market and social trends in other areas of our life. This can indeed be observed.

Prechter gives a wide variety of examples in his two-volume book *Socionomics: The Science of History and Social Prediction*. They come from all kinds of areas of our social life and range from popular music and fashion over the popularity of baseball and basketball to the election of political leaders, the outbreak of wars and nuclear testing. I would like to pick one of Prechter's studies, which in my opinion illustrates quite well this correlation between the stock market and popular trends.

Horror movies and Disney cartoons

Figure 38 shows the release dates of classic Disney cartoons and horror movies in the twentieth century compared to the movement of the Dow Jones Industrial Average. What is striking is the fact that Disney's cartoons were always extremely popular near stock market peaks and during bull market phases. At the Dow peak in the 1930s, Snow White and The Seven Dwarfs found a wide audience. During the long bull market of the 1950s and 1960s, Disney movies met with great popularity throughout that period, but then saw a sharp decline into the bear market of the 70s and 80s. It was not until the bull market of the 90s that Disney cartoons came back into fashion. In correlation with the stock market mania of the 90s they did so with a vengeance resulting in some of the biggest financial successes in Disney's history.

On the other hand, we can see that groundbreaking horror movies were never popular during bull markets. Their time came at stock market troughs and during bear markets. Following the crash of the early 1930s the now classic horror movies such as Frankenstein, Dracula, Dr. Jekyll & Mr. Hyde or King Kong were extremely popular. So was The Wolf Man in the middle of the 1940s. And the bear market of the 1970s and 80s saw another »Golden Age« for horror movies. What is not on the graph yet is the most recent period of popularity of horror movies. It started with the down movement of the stock market in 2000 and then again in 2008/2009 onwards, which has generated a flood of new and popular horror movies.

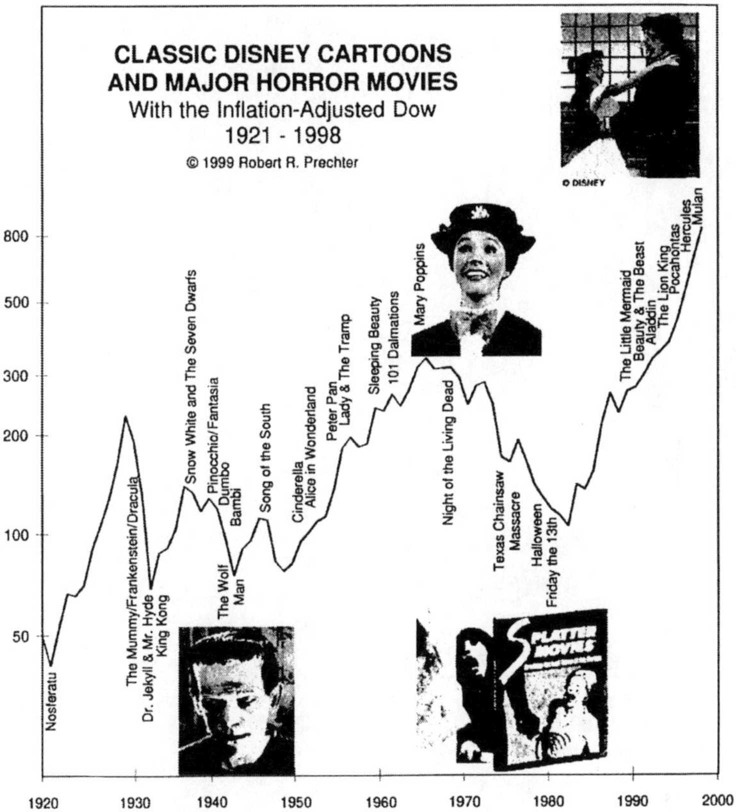

Figure 38: Movies and the stock market

Source: Prechter, Robert: The Wave Principle of Human Social Behavior and the New Science of Socionomics, 1999

I believe this example shows quite nicely how the both stock market and the popularity of movies go hand in hand. They both reflect social mood in terms of positive (Disney movies, bull market) and negative (horror movies, bear market) sentiment.

As mentioned above, many more such examples could be given. The length of hemlines follows the rhythm of the stock market (a fact which has been known for a long time) just as pop music or sports do (Figures 39 and 40) but to discuss them in detail would go beyond the scope of this book. What is important to recognize ist that social mood dominates all aspects of our social life and that the stock market is far from being the only manifestation of the Wave Principle.

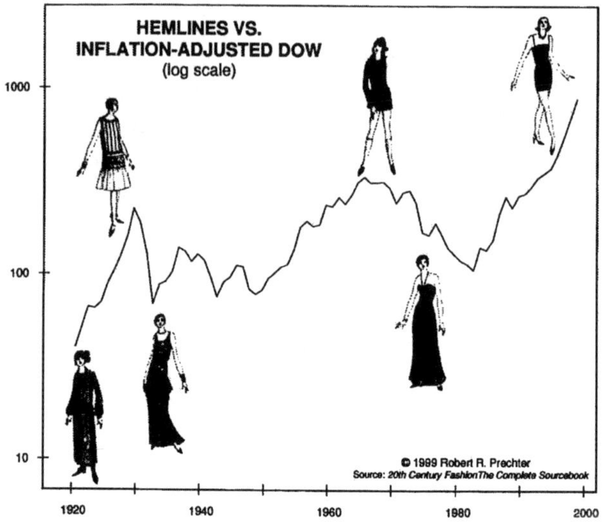

Figure 39: Hemlines and the Dow Jones

Source: Prechter, Robert: The Wave Principle of Human Social Behavior and the New Science of Socionomics, 1999

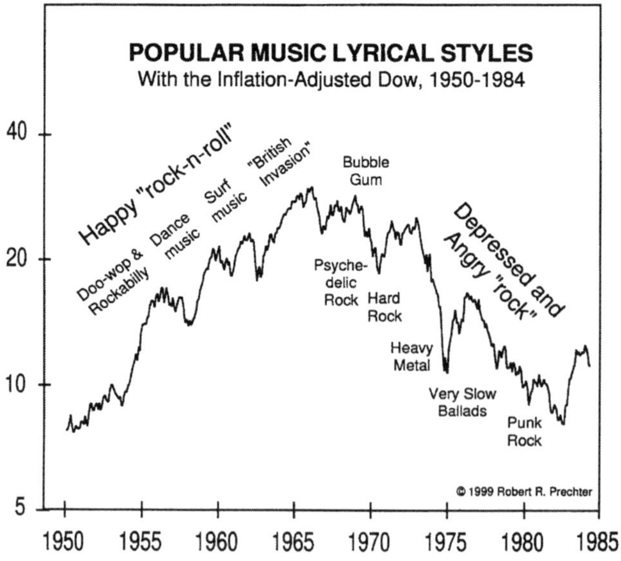

Figure 40: Popular music and the stock market

Source: Prechter, Robert: The Wave Principle of Human Social Behavior and the New Science of Socionomics, 1999

Historical impulsion

An important point to notice is that, on the one hand, social trends do follow the stock market, but that, on the other hand, most of them trail it in terms of time. The waves of most social trends lag behind the stock market's movements. This can best be seen in an area where people usually claim that the exact opposite is true. Figure 41 shows economic recessions and expansions in the twentieth century. What we can clearly see is that »the economic change does not precede and cause mood change; it follows mood change. In fact, the bigger the mood change, the bigger the effect.«[185] Again, this depends on the level of recursion on which it happens.
What you usually hear is that ›this and that economic development will have this and that effect on the stock market‹. The statistical data clearly refutes this notion.

The reason why most social trends lag behind the financial markets is, according to Prechter, that in most areas of social life it takes more time for social mood to be translated into actions than in the stock market.[186] In the stock market it does not take long to buy and sell stocks. A phone call or a

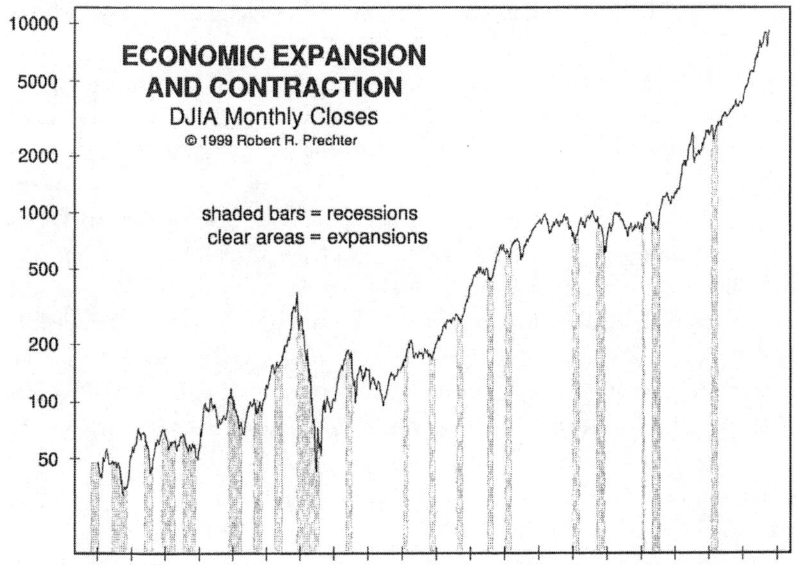

Figure 41: Economic expansions and contractions lag behind the stock market
Source: Prechter, Robert: The Wave Principle of Human Social Behavior and the New Science of Socionomics, 1999

mouse click suffices. But in areas such as politics or the economy or fashion, it takes longer to take appropriate action according to the mood one is in, or I had better say it takes longer for the effects of those actions to become apparent.

That most social trends trail the stock market is strong evidence for a point earlier made: That the Wave Principle is of endogenous origin. The statistical data, which Prechter presents, supports the view that the Wave pattern is independent and uninfluenced by outside effects. Contrary to the currently held belief, it seems that outside events have no impact on people's aggregate mood. It is social mood which drives history and becomes manifest in historical events. This is the socionomic paradigm:

»Events do not shape social mood; social mood shapes events. Mass psychological fluctuations are not simply correlated with mankind's actual progress and regress through history, but in fact are their engine. Collective mood shapes the character of social interaction, and thus of resulting actions and events.«[187]

This new paradigm completely changes the way that we look at things. Social mood shapes actions and events – not the other way around. It is a process which Prechter calls »historical impulsion«. The following comparison is meant to show how fundamentally different the socionomic view is from the standard view that we have today.[188]

Social mood is an indicator of the state of society on the aggregate. Because it follows the Wave Principle, the pattern can tell us what kind of actions and events we have to expect in the future. Just like the Wave pattern, »social mood is always in flux at all degrees of trend, moving toward one of the polar opposites in every conceivable area ...«.[189] This allows us to shift our point of view and look at events in a different way. Whenever something great occurs, be it positive or negative, people tend to look at it as a sign that this trend will last and even be amplified. From a socionomic point of view, the exact opposite is true. The more positive an event is, the greater the chance that a peak in the Wave pattern has been reached or is at least approaching and that, therefore, it is more likely that one will have to expect a reversal of the trend.

Socionomics, therefore, provides a fundamentally new perspective. It allows for a different view and a new orientation towards historical events and makes – for the first time ever – one more thing possible: the anticipation of future events.

The Standard View	The Socionomic Hypothesis
(exogenous cause)	**(endogenous cause)**
Social events determine the tenor of social mood	Social mood determines the tenor of social events
Examples	Examples
»Recession causes businessmen to be cautious.»	»Cautious businessmen cause recessions.»
»Talented leaders make the popularity happy.»	»A happy population makes leaders appear talented.»
»Epidemics cause people to be fearful and depressed.»	»Depressed and fearful people are susceptible to epidemics.»
»A rising stock market makes people increasingly optimistic.»	»Increasingly optimistic people make the stock market rise.»
»Scandals make people outraged.»	»Outraged people seek out scandals.»
»The availability of derivates fosters a desire to speculate.»	»A desire to speculate fosters the availability of derivates.»
»War makes people fearful and angry.»	»Fearful and angry people make war.»
»Happy music makes people smile.»	»People who want to smile choose happy music.»
»Nuclear bomb testing makes people nervous.»	»Nervous people test nuclear bombs.»

Anticipation and forecasting

Let us recapitulate briefly what has been stated so far. Socionomics is a science that examines social trends. These social trends reflect social mood and follow the Wave Principle. The Wave Principle is of endogenous origin, has a given recursive form and in addition to that is dominated by Fibonacci mathematics. With the right knowledge of the Wave Principle, therefore, it is possible to anticipate and forecast future developments to a certain extent. I am deliberately saying »to a certain extent« because forecasting on the basis of the Wave Principle will necessarily be probabilistic.

Society is a complex system. And, as we have seen, complex systems cannot be controlled in the sense that every detail and aspect of the system is under complete control. There are far too many variables in a complex system and the vast majority of them will never be known to us. In dealing with complex systems we are therefore restricted to the recognition of patterns, as Friedrich von Hayek explained.[190] We can only influence the big picture and our ability to »control« a system with a certain degree of complexity is restricted to the structure, the pattern. We can set out the rough lines but how the system will behave in detail remains in the dark and is not for us to manipulate. Such is the nature of a complex system – it is necessarily self-organizing.

The Wave Principle reflects this sort of abstraction as well. It is neither completely determined nor is it completely random. Hardly ever does it allow us to forecast any details. It gives us the chance to anticipate the structure and the pattern of the future, but what its specifics will be remains in the dark. Our ability to forecast the future is »only« probabilistic. What we are dealing with is propensities in the sense that the great philosopher Sir Karl Popper used the word.[191] Within certain restricting limits (such as the overall form in the Wave Principle) there are numerous propensities that could be realized but only one of them will be. Which one this will be depends on countless factors and variables and we can only try to anticipate it within the overall pattern. Indeed, every development in the system will further limit the number of possible outcomes and will tell us more about the future development. This means that anticipating and forecasting in complex systems is a continuous process[192] much as evolution is a continuous selection process.

I hope this makes clear that the opinion is wrong that complex systems – and therefore society – are entirely unpredictable. What is different from simple systems is the degree to which they are predictable. »The key to predicting formological systems is in their patterns.«[193]

It should also make clear that the prediction of complex systems is nothing which could ever be considered certain. Because we are dealing with probabilities, with propensities, there is always an uncertainty factor.

> »The Wave Principle guarantees reliable forecasting only of probabilities. It allows us to predict some aspects of the future and not others. For example, early in a new social mood trend, we can forecast society's coming character changes but not necessarily specific events.«[194]

Because of the general and probabilistic character of forecasting in complex systems, I much prefer the term »anticipation« to »forecast«, especially when we come to talk about legislative action for future events. Forecasting seems to come with a demand of certainty. The word anticipate on the other hand seems to me to express the kind of built-in uncertainty that comes naturally with predictions of any complex system.

Predictions about society, then, are possible. But we always need to be aware of the degree of specificity to which they are possible. This is something that shall concern us more when we move on to the question of how legislative assemblies could take action in regulating anticipated developments. However, it is important to understand that having too much confidence in specific forecasts is just as inappropriate as denying the possibility of future predictions altogether. As Prechter puts it: »Ultimately, then, we can say that laws of formological systems lead to utterly predictable results within the confines of probability statements.«[195]

3.2.3 Excursus

Existence of long waves

Waves and cycles can be found in many fields. They are a common phenomenon. Or I had better say: in many fields, the concept of waves and cycles is used as a tool to understand and explain the recurrence of certain patterns.

We are all familiar with cycles in nature, of course. The revolving of the earth around its own axis that leads to the night and day cycle; the revolving of the earth around the sun during the course of a year that leads to the seasons; the course of the moon around our earth that causes the tides. We could also speak of human life as a repeating cycle: one is born, goes from childhood to adolescence, then to maturity and senescence and eventually death. Meanwhile, a new generation grows up and the cycle repeats itself.

We take these cycles for granted. We do not question them because we can see them and they are part of our everyday lives. There are other cycles in nature that are not quite as obvious to us because they do not involve us. For example, we can find quite regular ups and downs in the population of many animals such as salmon, mice and lynxes, often linked to other species by a predator-prey balance. With trees, there regularly are periods of stronger and weaker growth as can be seen from the study of tree rings. Other examples include cycles in the concentration of ozone in our atmosphere, regular recurrences of diseases and epidemics and climate shifts from cold periods with ice ages to hotter and more humid periods.[196]

But these are simply examples of cycles in nature. What is more interesting for us, of course, are cycles in human social life. We can find quite a few examples here, too. I shall be focusing on cycles and waves dealt with in economics, as these are the best-studied examples. Besides, we shall see that most of them are not purely economic but are actually full-fledged social phenomena and that economists are simply the ones most aware of their existence.

Economic cycles

Cycle theories were prominent in economics – at times even dominant – during the first half of the last century. Then, after World War II, throughout the upswing and the economic growth period of the 1950s and 1960s, they came out of fashion and were almost completely forgotten. It was not until the unexpected downtrend in the 1970s that they were once again unearthed as a possible explanation of the sudden change of trend in the business world. Since then, cycles and long wave theories have enjoyed a strong revival and are still being discussed quite vividly.

One of the first to propose an economic cycle in 1860 was Clément Juglar who described the Juglar cycle named after him. Juglar tried to show that an economic crisis is only part of a much bigger cyclical movement of alternating prosperity and recession. He described the observed cycle empirically using statistical data both from the economy and from history to come up with a better understanding of the process. According to him this cyclical movement was a wave underlying the entire world economy lasting between seven and eleven years.[197]

Early works on cycles were also conducted by Van Gelderen (1913) and De Wolff (1924). Van Gelderen was probably the first to formulate and suggest a long wave hypothesis for the developed industrialized nations since the middle of the nineteenth century after having studied the movements of foreign exchange prices, interest rates and new issues, the tonnage of the cargo of ships and the production level. He came to the conclusion that besides a ten-year cycle there is also evidence for cyclical movements lasting several decades. De Wolff refined Van Gelderen's analysis and traced cycles back to the year 1825.[198]

Another scholar who described a somewhat shorter cycle averaging 40 months (3.3 years) was Joseph Kitchin in 1923. Kitchin believed it to be tied to fluctuations in prices, production, employment and a number of other factors.[199]

A longer wave was suggested by Nobel laureate Simon Kuznets. He claimed to have found a wave lasting 22 years on average. However, later investigations have found differing results so that now the Kuznets wave – also called long-swing – is said to have a length of 14 to 30 years.[200]

The father of the long wave was the Russian Nikolai Kondratieff. He first suggested the concept of a long wave as early as 1910, but it was not until 1922 that he published it after having started to work seriously on it in 1919. In his opinion, there are waves of 50 to 60 years underlying all economic (and social (!)) activity. One complete cycle has an up-wave and a down-wave, the up-wave usually averaging between 21 and 25 years with the downswing lasting a bit longer, about 29 to 32 years. According to Kondratieff, every wave shows more or less the same pattern, which means that there are similarities between the waves in terms of the stages that are discernible.[201]

The man who studied long waves and cycles most thoroughly and made these theories popular was the great Austrian economist Joseph A. Schumpeter. Schumpeter approached cycles in a rather historic and descriptive way as opposed to Kondratieff who did so mainly statistically. But they both came to the same conclusions. In his two-volume work Business Cycles[202], Schumpeter investigated mainly Kitchin as well as Juglar and Kondratieff cycles and the way in which they are related. In his opinion, each Kondratieff long wave is made up of five or six Juglars and several Kitchins. He did not find the pattern all the time but each time that it was missing, there was some special factor involved such as a war for example.

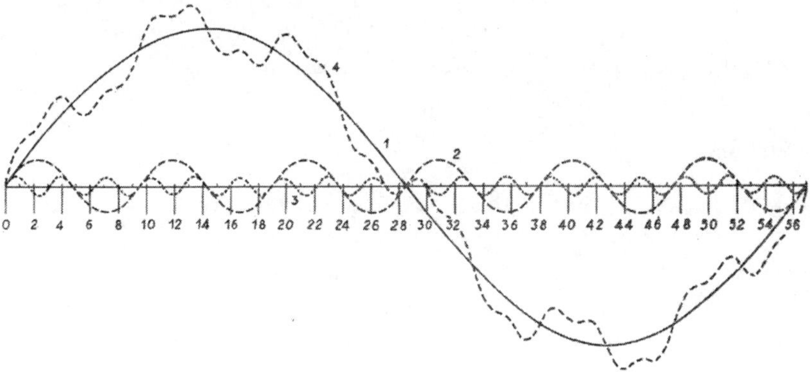

Figure 42: The combination of three waves. 1: Kondratieff cycle; 2: Juglar cycle; 3: Kitchin cycle; 4: combination of all three cycles.
Source: J. A. Schumpeter, Business Cycles, p. 223.

Although most authors focus on economic aspects and emphasize economic triggers and consequences, it is widely acknowledged that cycles and waves are not just economic but general social phenomena. They are a »weltgesellschaftliches«[203] phenomenon that includes cultural, economic, political, demographical and psychological factors.[204] All of them play a role and it would be wrong to exclude or ignore one of them. Kondratieff's theory already acknowledged this in that it was based on the assumption that there is a complete interrelationship between social and political developments, financial behavior, economics, wars and revolutions. We are therefore right to assume that there are long waves in human psychology just as there are long waves in the economy. They cannot be separated from each other. The key to the understanding of cycles and waves will have to be an interdisciplinary approach.[205]

Among scholars there is no agreement on whether there are long waves and cycles or not. Some doubt their existence altogether.[206] However, what is undoubted is that certain events and patterns throughout history keep recurring. We might not have complete explanations for these phenomena and their background and mechanics might remain a secret to us. Many factors might contribute to their development with crowd psychology being just one of them. But theories including long waves and cycles offer an explanation that allows us to put things into perspective and provide us with an orientation for the future. Thus, such theories are helpful tools against which to judge our actions. Such tools are of tremendous importance for our individual as well as economic and political decisions because these decisions need to be different depending on whether a current trough is the low of a short cycle or whether it is the much longer lasting low of a long wave which requires a different kind of measures and actions.

Determinism?

A common misconception that leads people to reject the mere thought of the existence of cycles and waves is that if they are acknowledged it would mean to accept that everything that happens is determined in advance and that the human being is simply a feather blown about by the wind and unable to influence his or her own destiny. Let us call it the »determinism vs. free will problem«.

At first glance, the notion of waves – especially long waves -, indeed, seems to logically imply a deterministic worldview. If there were a continuous up and down that is certain to occur and cannot be changed or influenced by us, then our lives and fates would not be controlled by us but would be subject to other forces beyond our reach. Hence, the future would not be open and free for us to create and shape but instead would be predetermined. The individual would not be master of his or her fate; free will would be an illusion.

In the social sciences it is above all economists who have concerned themselves with theories relating to waves and cycles. They have done so for most of a century. In economics, too, one of the main arguments against long cycles is the determination argument.

The interesting thing is that it is only the opponents who interpret wave theories in this way. Practically no one among the supporters of the idea that long waves and cycles exist thinks of it as deterministic.[207] They think of it as probabilistic.

Waves and cycles are analytic and forecasting tools that are based on pattern recognition. Their pattern repeats, yet neither the amplitude nor the period of time over which they develop are fixed or remain constant. Due to the complexity of the interconnections of our economic, political, technological and socio-cultural worlds, it cannot be expected that cycles develop in a completely regular fashion like a clockwork mechanism. They should always be looked at as systems that show probabilistic and more or less asymmetrical and irregular behavior[208] whose pattern, however, is repetitive.

There is another important point to note. Waves and cycles are phenomena of aggregates, of collectives, for probabilities have to do with averages. Scholars who work with cycle theories and make predictions based on them do not make any statements about individuals.[209] They make a statement about how a number of people will behave on the aggregate.

This leads to two conclusions. First, long wave and cycle theories are working tools to better understand, explain and foresee certain recurring events and developments. Cycles and long waves are not strictly regular phenomena but behave according to probability fluctuations. When some of them are depicted as sine or cosine curves then these are merely illustrations aimed at helping to understand better where in the pattern something occurs. So, even the phenomena themselves are not deterministic. Second, as long waves and cycles deal with explanations and forecasts of aggregates and collectives, as they show properties of crowd behavior, no statements are made about what any individual might do at any given moment. Nothing is said about specific outcomes and events. Waves and cycles provide an orientation as to the overall development. As Carlota Perez of Cambridge University puts it: »Historical regularities are not a blueprint; they only indicate likelihood.«[210] Whether there will be war or peace, whether there will be higher or lower interest rates or whether someone will buy vanilla or chocolate ice cream is not something that is predetermined but depends on countless variables within the complexity of our world.

The pattern of a wave or a cycle restricts the possible number of outcomes of the overall trend and development. So there is something deterministic in that but it does not restrict the individual's will. It leaves the individual free to act according to his or her own will (although many might not because they succumb to the suction of the crowd). Knowing the pattern can, on the contrary, enable us to be even freer since we can consciously understand what is going on. We can benefit from this knowledge by positioning ourselves within the trend so as to be able to live according to our own ideas and wishes.

Another strong argument against determinism comes from the great philosopher Sir Karl Popper. In his book *A world of Propensities* he explains why, in his opinion, »determinism is simply wrong« and why »all traditional arguments for determinism have become spurious«.[211] According to Popper, a propensity is the property of a situation to produce a particular result. It is more than the possibility that something might happen. Rather, propensities are realities; forces that strive to fulfill themselves; forces that are immanent in a situation. Just whether they do or do not fulfill themselves depends on the circumstances, i. e. different situations favor different propensities.[212]

In physics we can sometimes keep situations stable or we can recreate them time and again. This means that potentially any propensity immanent in the situation will eventually fulfill itself if we allow for enough time. In our real world situations are subject to constant change and with them their propensities change. Actually, we change them ourselves through our preferences, our hopes, wishes, dreams and theories. Thus, past situations do not determine the future. They cause changing propensities, which influence future conditions but do not determine them in any specific way. The future is not determined but open.[213]

Orientation

We should look at cycles and waves as factors that influence a situation and therefore favor certain propensities over others. They limit the number of propensities that can fulfill themselves. However, this number is still huge. And although wave and cycle patterns can, therefore, not teach us anything specific and detailed about the future, nothing about particular events and actions, they provide us with a tool for the anticipation of society's development at large. They provide us with an orientation towards the future. They give us the chance to anticipate changes in social trends and prepare for them. And even tough they only indicate probabilities, the perspective provided by them is better than anything we have today and can lead to real progress in legislative activity.

Part IV – Preparation

4. Preparing Society: Transforming legislative action

We have seen how the time lag between societal developments and legislative action can be dangerous for the stability of society. If changes and developments are not anticipated and, thus, no preparations are made to cushion and absorb them, situations are created in which possible negative and harmful consequences of such developments cannot be avoided anymore. Such situations can be threatening to the peace and order of a society and might, in the worst case, lead a society to the edge of breakdown.

The source of such changes are crowd psychological processes that suffuse society like invisible rivers and ebb and flow together with the waves of social mood. Sometimes change is only moderate and, although legislative action lags behind, the negative consequences of this delay are insignificant. But when extreme changes in social mood occur they can manifest themselves in such infamous crowd phenomena as wars, riots, revolutions and manias. When this happens, it is too late to avoid damage: people get hurt and assets are destroyed.

Such advanced crowd phenomena need to be prevented as they cannot be controlled, except by force. They are destructive and most threatening to social stability. Prevention means that they need to be anticipated so measures can be taken in advance. Key to this is the knowledge and understanding of basic crowd phenomena – as they are the breeding ground for advanced ones – and this is what Socionomics provides. Basic crowd phenomena can be controlled; they can be steered, channeled and mitigated so that advanced phenomena cannot develop in the first place.

To do this effectively, our law-making institutions urgently have to make use of the insights that we have gained in crowd psychology, Socionomics and managerial cybernetics. Legislation must be transformed from a lagging mechanism into an anticipating one.

Until this day there has never been legislation of this kind. And, as we shall see, there are problems which make it almost impossible for an anticipatory mechanism to be built into today's system without fundamental reform and restructuring. The ideas laid out here might therefore be called »utopian« by some, but it is my conviction that they point in the direction that we must follow if progress is to be achieved. I understand what follows as a thought experiment, a rough suggestion of what a reform of our legislatures might look like.

4.1 Society as a Viable System

If any system that means to be viable must show the structure of the Viable System Model (VSM), as we have seen, then, clearly, so does a society. For the protection of the life and liberty of the people and of our fundamental values we need a functioning society – we need a viable society. Today, it is society which supplies the individual with the most basic goods that it needs to be viable itself such as food, shelter and security. Society is the environment in which the individual exists and without which it cannot be.[214]

It has already been mentioned that the concept of viability can mean different things. A system can be viable and merely survive. At the same time, a system can be viable and prosper. Whether it is the one or the other depends on many different variables and conditions. What is clear, however, is that in order for a system to have the possibility to prosper in the long term all the five different subsystems of the VSM need to be well developed and functioning.

It is open to discussion whether a war, a civil war or a revolution constitutes the breakdown of a society with the complete loss of viability. After all, in a way society abides. But when thousands or even millions of people die, then this constitutes a system failure in any case. And this is strong evidence that certain necessary subsystems are at least underdeveloped. The ones most often observed to be underdeveloped are Systems 2 and 4.

The topic of this book is not the implementation of the Viable System Model to a society as a whole.[215] I will, therefore, get directly to the point which concerns us most and which is, as we have already seen, System 4. When events such as wars, revolutions or manias occur then this is often due to an underdevelopment of System 4. As we have seen in Part II, System 4 is responsible for the supervision of what is to come. It has to concern itself with possible future environments and developments for which the system needs to prepare. If developments and changes that lead to a war, a revolution or a stock market mania are not anticipated, then this task has not been fulfilled satisfactorily. In case of war, this is not necessarily so, of course. A country can be attacked by another country and simply has to defend itself. This does not in itself mean that its System 4 is underdeveloped. However, this is so only if it is found prepared. Otherwise, it would be a System-4 failure.

In our modern states, System 4 is usually poorly developed. This does not mean that there are no elements performing System 4 tasks. There are, of course, already diverse System 4 elements in our modern societies. Many of them will have other functions as well and their System-4 function will be just one task among others. It is important to realize that hardly ever will we find an element in a system that is exclusively attributed one function.

For example, the Prime Minister of the United Kingdom has many functions from the point of view of the Viable System Model: As the head of the executive he clearly has a System-3 function, as he needs to deal with present problems of his country. But he is also a figure that has an integrating effect and strengthens the cohesion and identity of the United Kingdom. Thus, he performs a System-5 function (the most prominent System-5 element being the Queen, of course). Moreover, he needs to concern himself with the future of the country and with influences from outside. Whenever he turns to such issues, he becomes part of System 4.

So we may detect System-4 functions in many individuals, organizations and institutions of society. To name but a few prominent ones: the ministry of foreign affairs with its embassies and consulates, intelligence agencies, governmental think tanks and committees dedicated to foreign affairs and future issues, universities, research and science departments, and the military. There are others. And they do not need to be official institutions. Private institutions and organizations can serve System-4 purposes just as well as official ones. Think about all the research departments of private companies or environmental organizations. They are all dedicated to future issues that might confront society even if they might not be dedicated directly to the service of society as a whole.

But even though we have all these System-4 elements, System 4 is still underdeveloped. There are two reasons for this in my opinion. First, System-4 functions are missing where they are most needed: in legislature. Actually, as we shall see, most legislative bodies are organized in a way that prevents them from performing System-4 functions even if they wanted to. Second, there is no »Focus«, as Stafford Beer calls it, i. e. there is no place where all the System-4 data is gathered and transformed into information so that it can be used.[216] Let us now have a look at the System-4 function of legislature. The »Focus« will concern us when we look at the elements that an anticipatory mechanism might need.

4.2 The System-4 Function of the legislature

It was already mentioned that we will hardly find any elements in a system that perform solely one function from the point of view of the Viable System. This holds true for the legislature as well. Just as the other two powers of our modern states, the executive and the judicative, it actually performs several functions in terms of the five subsystems.

There is its System-3 function: Many laws, indeed most laws nowadays, are dedicated to the regulation and steering (and unfortunately detailed control) of present issues. Be it tax law, civil law or administrative law, most matters regulated are matters of present concern. Most laws are passed for present problems or problems that are almost certain to occur because the conditions are already there. This here and now focus is typical for System 3.

There is also the very important System-5 function of legislative assemblies. In most countries this is some kind of representative body that decides on a constitution and alterations to it and thereby decides on the fundamental principles that are to guide a society. Although the constitution is made to survive parliament and, then, itself takes on a System-5 function of central importance, it is the legislature that makes the decision in the first place and thereby performs a System-5 task. But even when it comes to the passing of »regular« laws the legislative assembly takes on a System-5 responsibility. The decision, which law is to be passed and which is not, is part of System 5. All the work prior to it – the preparatory work, committee meetings, the questioning of experts, the support functions of the administration – might belong to the realm of a different system, but as soon as a bill is sent to the floor and it comes to voting, i. e. to making a decision, representatives perform a classical System-5 function.

Most pertinent to our discussion is the legislature's System-4 function. I believe that it is absolutely necessary for the legislature to play an active part in System 4. The members of a legislative assembly are elected as representatives of the people. They are thereby entrusted with the welfare of the country and of society. The responsibility for the most fundamental decisions for the present and the future lies in their hands. One of their fundamental tasks must be to prepare society for tomorrow, i. e. to legislate for the future. They must think ahead, try to anticipate what it might be with which society will have to put up and find solutions for it. The preparation of society can only take place in legislature. Of course, actual measures will at some point be taken by the executive, but government action of any kind must necessarily be based on law in a modern state founded on the rule of law – and law is made by the legislature. It is therefore necessary for the legislature to play an active part in supervising and investigating the future and thereby form the core of System 4.

As was mentioned above, legislative assemblies are by far not the only element in society that performs a System-4 function. Especially in terms of the actual outlook and anticipating process there may be institutions and organizations that are just as important as a legislative body. But the legislature is the only place where information and knowledge gathered about the future can be transformed into preparatory action, i. e. anticipatory laws. Only if available information about the future is translated into laws can there be an anticipatory regulative steering effect. Otherwise, we might as well refrain from spending money on information gathering for it is useless unless this information is transformed into action. So no matter how elaborate our System 4 is, it is not good enough unless we have a working System-4 function of our legislative bodies.

Now, laws can have far-reaching effects. Of course, there is a constant debate as to the extent to which it is possible to steer society by means of law.[217] But there is no doubt that law can have a steering effect. I would distinguish between two categories of steering influences that law can have on society:

1. Law can be normative. In this case it says how something should be. It does not merely describe a fact or observed state but tries to bring about what is desired and prevent what is undesired. It makes a general decision about the value of something.
2. Law can be (merely) regulative. Of course, in such a case the regulation will always occur in accordance with normative rules set up in advance by the law. But in its regulative function the law does not come up with new statements about how something should be but merely tries to channel developments so they fit in with the overall (normative and actual) present societal structure.

Our main question concerns future events and developments. So in terms of the future, the law in its normative steering function shapes or at least tries to shape the future. This is more of a System-5 function. In its regulative steering function the law cushions and mitigates the future. This is a genuine and fundamental task of System 4 as it is concerned with things to come that the system itself cannot shape. As we have seen, according to Socionomics, the waves of human social behavior cannot be influenced. They simply happen because they are of endogenous origin. For this reason, our focus needs to be on the regulative steering function of the law and therefore of legislative action.

This function is, as has already been mentioned, clearly underdeveloped. It is not that the regulative steering function as such is underdeveloped. On the contrary, we are faced with drastic overregulation.[218] More and more areas of our lives are dominated by legal rules as governments try to regulate every detail of society. But this overregulation focuses on present issues and problems in the sense of a System-3 function. Very little thought is given to the question of how we could regulate things to come before they actually happen. Yet this is what System 4 has to do and this is why the System-4 function of our legislative assemblies is strongly underdeveloped.

Without assuming the responsibility of trying to prepare society for the future, a legislative assembly does not fulfill its function. It must be at the center of interest of a body of representatives to see what can be done to not just reestablish peace and order of a society but to protect them by establishing safeguards prior to potentially threatening developments.

4.3 Obstacles to effective System-4 legislation

It would be nice if we could just say: »Problem recognized. Dear representatives, from now on, please start thinking ahead.« Unfortunately it is not that easy. Nowadays, there are mainly two problems that prevent our parliaments from even being considered capable of performing such a task effectively. These two problems – interconnected as they are – are immanent in our republican system:

- The legislature's dependence on interest groups
- The legislature's short-term orientation

4.3.1 Dependence on interest groups[219]

One of the greatest evils that our governmental systems have brought about is the dependence on interest groups of whoever it is that wants to get elected.[220] Parties need the support of unions, of the economic and industrial lobbies, of women, of ethnic minorities, of the churches, of the farmers, etc. They need votes to get elected. And how do they get these votes? By pleasing people and by making promises to support them and give them what they want once they are in power.

Thus, whoever wins the election is necessarily forced to satisfy their supporters unless they want to lose their credibility and the chance to govern for more than just one term. They cannot do what is necessary and right for society as a whole. They need to do what is necessary to assure continued support by the majority.

The reason for all this is to be found in the system itself. What we have today in most countries is unlimited government.[221] It is widely assumed that since what we have today is democratic government, there do not need to be any limitations to that government. At least in practice this is what we have. So the executive is usually part of the legislature (there are exceptions such as Switzerland and the United States). Thus, when a party comes to power, it automatically has two powers: First, it is given control of the resources of society and second, it is given the power to alter the law. The combination of these two powers allows it actually to satisfy the interest groups that supported it and this alone is the reason why there is lobbying at all. If these two powers were separated, lobbying would not exist since it would be useless: Those who make the laws would not be able to hand out favors, and those able to give hand-outs would not have the power to influence the law:

»To place those who ought to define what is right in a position in which they can maintain themselves only by giving their supporters what they want, is to place at their disposal all the resources of society for whatever purpose they think necessary to keep them in power«.[222]

Today, this is what the situation is like, unfortunately, and it is because of this that governments become intrinsically »corrupt«.

»This domination of government by coalitions of organized interests (when they were first observed they were generally described as ›sinister interests‹) is usually regarded by the outsider as an abuse, or even a kind of corruption. It is, however, the inescapable result of a system in which government has unlimited powers to take whatever measures are required to satisfy the wishes of those on whose support it relies.[223]

This legalized corruption is not the fault of the politicians; they cannot avoid it if they are to gain positions in which they can do any good. It becomes a built-in feature of any system in which majority support authorizes a special measure assuaging particular discontent«.[224]

This »corruption«, i. e. the dependence of the government on interest groups, is therefore one of the main reasons why System-4 issues are neglected. Politics are necessarily governed by the attempt to secure the support of the majority by satisfying voters and supporters. There simply remains no room and no time to deal with future issues and developments that might affect the whole of society. Individual interests are necessarily the focus of politicians and their demand for satisfaction absorbs all the energy and resources that could otherwise be invested in the reflection about society's future challenges. Thus, the System-4 function of our legislative assemblies is neglected and remains underdeveloped.

4.3.2 Short-term orientation

»... True legislation is thus essentially a task requiring the long view...«[225]

Most legislative assemblies are elected for a relatively short period of time. Often it is four years. Sometimes it is a little more as in the case of the members of the Senate of the United States, who are elected for six years.[226] Nevertheless, even six years is a short time given the time that it takes to get used to things and learn how everything works. Moreover, during the last year of their term, representatives are often far from effective and their minds are concentrated on matters such as getting laws passed, as they need to be concerned about getting reelected. So the term of office itself and their dependence on reelection already forces representatives to have a short-term focus.

Politicians' dependence on interest groups has already been mentioned. This dependence also means that, to get enough support to get elected or reelected, representatives necessarily have to deal with the problems that people have now. Individuals as well as interest groups are focused on their present problems that they want to be solved. It is not about long-term developments, which might affect the whole of society. It is about what troubles them now. The farmers need subsidies now, the unions want better work conditions, fewer work hours and higher salaries now, industry needs financial support and lower taxes now, and so on.

In a situation such as this there necessarily must be a focus on short-term goals and problems. There cannot be a long-term orientation. If a representative were to tackle problems that are in the future and if these problems in addition to that were uncertain and there were only a probability of them becoming reality (as Socionomics implies), he would hardly find enough support among his constituents as well as among his fellow representatives to both get a bill passed and then get reelected at the end of his term.

4.3.3 Hayek's constitutional model[227]

The dependence on interest groups of those who are charged with the making of the law and their focus on short-term problems and goals are the two big obstacles that render impossible an effective System-4 function of the legislature. The source of all this, as we have seen, is that the power to legislate and the control over society's resources are placed in the same hands. Before an effective anticipatory mechanism can be introduced into the legislature, these problems need solving.

A constitutional model that could help solve these problems is the one proposed by Friedrich von Hayek in the third volume of his series Law, Legislation and Liberty. In his work Hayek starts out from the conviction that the »attempt to secure individual liberties by constitutions has evidently failed«[228] since governments all over the world have continuously managed to obtain powers in spite of and even with the help of constitutions that should actually have served to deny them these powers. According to Hayek, the confidence in the will of the majority has led to unlimited government, which is the opposite of what constitutional government actually means.

In his opinion, the source of all evil is a wrong understanding of what law actually means[229] and what it should be and, something that I have already mentioned, the combination of the power to make law and having the resources of society at one's disposal, i. e. the making of law and the directing of government. The consequence of this is that today's representatives and governments are losing their independence as they become increasingly dependent on individual interests for support and the use of legislative means for specific purposes instead of for the common good.

The logical consequence for Hayek is to separate the two powers and propose a model in which there is a Legislative Assembly and a Governmental Assembly. The legislative assembly would be entrusted with the making of the law, i. e. the passing of general rules of conduct applicable to:

»an indefinite number of unknown future instances, to serve the formation and preservation of an abstract order whose concrete contents were unpredictable, but not the achievement of particular concrete purposes, and finally to exclude all provisions intended or known to affect principally particular identifiable individuals or groups«.[230]

The governmental assembly would more or less look like the parliamentary bodies and governments that we have today. Within the scope of the rules laid down by the legislative assembly it would be completely free to do what it thinks necessary to organize the governmental apparatus and to decide on how to use the resources available to it. To supervise the separation of the two assemblies and make sure that their respective tasks, duties and rights remain clearly segregated, a special court would have to be established, which Hayek calls the constitutional court.

In terms of the composition and election of the two assemblies there would have to be different regulations, as the members might otherwise come from the same pool of people, which would create the risk that the current entanglement might simply continue. Therefore, Hayek suggests that the members of the legislative assembly be elected for a period of fifteen years after which they would not be re-eligible. Moreover, there should be a representation according to age groups to reflect the different dominant opinions in society. The election processes and regulations that we have today could continue to apply for the election and composition of the governmental assembly. There could be parties, a majority government and an opposition and the length of the term of office could stay the same as well.

We cannot go into the details of Hayek's model here. But I wanted to give an overview because the problems that Hayek sees with today's system in general, such as the dependence on interest groups and the prevailing shortsightedness are, in my opinion, also the cause for the lack of an effective anticipatory mechanism of the legislature. And the remedy that Hayek suggests could help pave the way for the introduction of such a mechanism.

I am not saying that Hayek's constitutional model can solve all the problems of today's system. But it addresses the very problem. And if we ever are to have a legislative body that, besides taking on present issues and problems, also considers it its duty to deal with the long-term prospect of society and is able to free itself from the needs and wants of individual interests for the sake of the whole, we have to find a new two-chamber model in which the power to pass laws and the power to control society's resources are separated.

The obstacles to an effective anticipatory mechanism of our legislatures are tremendous. And, of course, it would be utopian to think that our democratic model could simply be restructured. We are so used to today's structure and it is so anchored in our thinking and our republican system that it might first even have to fail completely once more before a reform is possible. But to state it clearly: I consider any attempt to make our legislatures more future-oriented useless unless these problems are solved first. Representatives are to be made independent of interests other than the ones of society as a whole and they are to be enabled to take a long-term view. Otherwise, there can be no serious talk of an anticipatory legislative function.

What follows now is a suggestion of what an anticipatory mechanism might look like and what elements it might have to contain. I do not claim completeness for the following thoughts but consider it a rough outline, which will certainly need further refining in the future.

4.4 Elements of an anticipatory mechanism for legislative assemblies

Let us suppose we could overcome the problems just discussed. We would then maybe have two chambers of representatives, one of which would be entrusted with legislation proper, i. e. the making and shaping of the law, and the other would be given control of the resources of society (whether the lawgiving assembly should be divided once more as is common today is not relevant here). The legislative assembly would only have the power to pass laws but would be unable to execute them. The governmental assembly on the other hand would have to execute the laws passed by the legislative assembly but would have no possibility whatsoever to alter any of these laws. Thus, dependence on individual interests would vanish, as any attempt to influence either chamber of representatives would be a waste of time in terms of achieving a particular goal.

At the same time, the term of office of the representatives in the legislative assembly would be prolonged. The representatives would maybe serve one single term (thus being independent of re-election) of maybe ten to fifteen years. This would give them the opportunity to really focus on trying to solve the problems which society faces without their minds being distracted by other issues, which are of importance only to their political career.

The way would then be open to the implementation of an effective System-4 function of the legislative assembly, as the sole focus on short-term issues would be eliminated. This should lead to the incorporation of questions concerning the future of society and to the possibility of anticipatory legislative action by the legislature.

It should be clear why we are focusing on the anticipatory function of the legislative assembly and not of the governmental assembly. We are trying to find answers to the question of how law's delay compared with societal changes and developments can be overcome and how it might be possible to legally regulate such changes and developments before they happen and possibly show harmful effects. Therefore, we necessarily need to look at the body that is responsible for lawmaking. The governmental assembly might well have important tasks with System-4 character but, as it is not able to pass new laws, it cannot be our focus. This must be the legislative assembly.

Bearing all this in mind, we now need to look at the elements that are needed inside and around the legislature for an effective anticipatory mechanism.

4.4.1 Administration

It is clear that prior to the passing of a law there is a rather long process, which involves the collecting of information, the consulting of experts, the considering of alternatives, the formulating of drafts, etc. It is also clear that this cannot all be done by the representatives themselves. They need support in all these matters.

Today, whether we like it or not, the large majority of laws is prepared by the administration, i. e. the different departments and ministries. Civil servants write the laws and often representatives do not even read them anymore. There simply is no time to study all the proposed bills, as there are far too many areas nowadays which our governments consider necessary regulating.

This is something that needs to be changed if we are to give corruption by interest groups no chance. If we were to separate the two powers and still allow the executive's administration to prepare the laws for the legislative assembly we would again expose the governmental assembly to the kind of influence by individual interests that we have today, as the executive, via its administration, would then have a rather large say in the making of the law.

There can be only one consequence to this: The legislative assembly needs an administration of its own. This sounds horrifying. After all, as citizens we are already confronted with a huge governmental apparatus that exhibits an ever-increasing degree of bureaucracy. The last thing that we need is a doubling of that. But I do not believe that this would be necessary. I believe that there is no need for such a huge bureaucratic apparatus whatsoever. But even if, as today's administration does all the administrative work for the executive and all the preparing of the laws to be passed as well, some of that capacity could simply be transferred to the legislature. Administration could be split and one half would be assigned to the legislative assembly while the other remains with the governmental assembly.

The legislature would then have an administration of its own. Its character would of course change completely. It would not be involved at all in executing laws anymore. Its sole business would be legislative issues, i. e. the revision and preparation of laws.

4.4.2 Lookout staff

It was mentioned above that the legislature has different functions in terms of the Viable System Model. Apart from a System-4 function there is also its System-3 function. These two functions are also functions of the administration of the legislature as it does all the preparatory work for the legislative assembly. As we have seen, System 4 and System 3 are opposed to each other, as their foci are the opposite.[231] For this reason I would consider it wise to have an administrative staff that concerns itself with either System-4 or with System-3 questions, but not with both. We would then have experts for present issues and we would have what you could call »lookout« staff that only deals with future questions. Lookout staff would have to focus on genuinely future issues and future problems and developments. It would have to collect the relevant information; it would need to deal with possible scenarios and possible events; it would need to consider changing trends and what it might mean for society.

Of course, work of this sort is already being done by Intelligence Agencies, security departments, military institutions and think tanks of all kinds.

Environmental monitoring and strategic planning are necessarily part of the program of such organizations, but they are so far not part of legislature. They are usually part of the executive and it often seems as if they were actually working against the legislature and as if they were not organizations serving the welfare of society. With the remodeling of the two chambers and the setting up of a System-4 function within the legislative assembly, this kind of thinking would necessarily have to become part of legislature's work as well. Therefore, committees, counseling bodies or special agencies would become necessary that supply the legislature with the kind of information needed. Whether new ones would have to be set up or whether the existing ones would suffice is a question that can remain open here. I personally do not think that it would be enough to simply restructure the ones that we have. In any case as part of the legislature's administration we would need a body of people for doing this kind of work and bringing strategic thinking to bear in legislative work.

There is another advantage to the division of the administration into System-3 and System-4 staff. If there are experts for the two tasks and people who focus on only one perspective, the chance of them having requisite variety to absorb the variety generated in Systems 3 and 4 is greater in my opinion. A lot of the variety generated might be absorbed by the staff prior to representatives dealing with the issues that arise. Thereby, representatives might be better able to focus on the important things and on monitoring the interaction of present and future perspectives.

If administrative staff should be assigned different tasks, since there are different functions to be fulfilled, why should not the same be done with the legislative assembly itself, i. e. the representatives? After all, the argument for the administrative staff was that legislature overall has System-3 and System-4 functions. It would only be logical then to split tasks among representatives as well. The reason why this must not be done is that the legislature's representatives fulfill a System-5 function at the same time but the legislature's administration does not. This means that the decision on and the responsibility for the laws passed and the balance of present and future focus lies with the representatives – and with the representatives only. If there were to be a division into System-3 and System-4 representatives, everyone would consider his own domain a priority and vote accordingly. This must not happen. The legislative assembly's concern needs to be the sake of the whole at all times.

4.4.3 Committees

I believe there should be special strategic legislative committees dealing with future issues and developments. Such committees should be permanent because, as we have seen, strategic planning is a continuous process. The concept of a committee is nothing new, of course. Committees are standard nowadays in all legislative assemblies. Therefore, it will not be necessary to elaborate on this extensively. One thing that I find important, however, is that a large number of representatives should be involved in such a committee. After all, a strategic committee would not specialize in a particular issue such as taxes or foreign policy but would deal with future developments in general. So the more representatives are able to participate the better. For this reason there should maybe be several strategic legislative committees and special sessions between them would have to take place every now and then to synchronize their knowledge and findings.

It might prove helpful for committees to have some kind of »decision platform«, i. e. a place where data is transformed into information and where an environment is provided that helps make the right decisions. Such a place could be Stafford Beer's so-called »Operations Room«, which we shall have a look at shortly.

4.4.4 Channels to other System-4 parts

It has already been mentioned that there are many institutions and organizations other than the legislature and its administration that perform System-4 tasks. The knowledge and the information available in such places need to be accessible to the legislature. Only this way can it be guaranteed that there will be a sound informational basis upon which to base new laws. This means that channels to such authorities as intelligence agencies, think tanks and military institutions need to be established. I picture it like a spider's web: From all different System-4 institutions there are strings running to the center, which is the System-4 headquarters of the legislature. The place where all the information is gathered could again be the Operations Room.

4.4.5 Information

For an efficient anticipatory function of the legislature a special kind of information is required. As we have already seen it is not enough simply to look at present problems, extrapolate them into the future and then try to find a cure. Legislatures today are doing just that and it makes the law lag behind. We need information that is future-oriented.

For true anticipation of the possible (or even probable) future, what we need is something that tells us how a trend will develop, i. e. when it might change, what its character might be and what kind of actions and events we might therefore have to expect. The study of long waves and cycles could provide just that. We have seen that wave theories can be helpful tools when it comes to understanding society's development and gaining an orientation regarding the future.

The information gained is – like the waves themselves – of a probabilistic nature. This means that we can never be entirely certain how a trend will develop and nothing can be said about any specifics that might happen during the development of the trend. But the pattern of the waves might let us anticipate the future course to a certain degree. And for legislation, this is already great progress as it makes a difference in terms of laws passed if it can be predicted whether current bad times are due to a wave trough that only lasts a short period of time or whether they need to be expected to continue. This is where Socionomics comes in. The socionomic approach is perfect for use as a tool within the System-4 mechanism of the legislature.

However, for information to be as accurate as possible, the different wave theories should be combined and applied together. They could be used to test each other. If there is a probable turning point in the Elliott Wave pattern, but no other cycle indicates such a turning point, then one had best be careful. If, on the other hand, the Elliott Wave pattern as well as the Kondratieff and the Kuznets wave call for a turning in the trend, it is an important clue as to the future development.

In this way, the study of social waves driven to a considerable degree by crowd psychological factors offers a unique approach to the anticipation of the future social climate. This knowledge can be used in legislation as an orientation point when passing laws applicable to future issues.

Expertise

I believe that representatives should have a basic understanding of Socionomics. They should know what it is, how it works, what it can do and especially also what it cannot do. If laws are to be passed based on socionomic foresight and implications, representatives should be familiar with the socionomic way of thinking. I doubt, though, that they can be required to become experts in it. Actually, I do not think that they should be. To provide experts is the job of the administration.

Among the administrative lookout staff there need to be experts in Socionomics. They need to understand the crowd psychological mechanisms on which it is founded; they need to understand Fibonacci mathematics and fractal geometry. I believe this is indispensable for the right kind of information to be gathered and for it to be interpreted correctly. Moreover, as we have seen in the chapter on Socionomics, the application of the theory is far from simple as we are dealing not with certainties but with probabilities. An in-depth understanding of the Wave Principle and its structure is therefore necessary to correctly handle the theory and anticipate future developments.

Sociometrics[232]

In Part I we saw why linear extrapolation of present trends and problems is no help in anticipating upcoming developments and that it can, and at some point must, lead to wrong conclusions about the future. For true anticipation of the possible (or even probable) future, what we need is something that tells us how a trend will develop, i.e. when it might change, what its character might be and what kind of actions and events we might therefore have to expect.

Socionomics states that social mood is endogenous and follows a pattern, which takes the shape of the Wave Principle. The place where we can most easily observe the development of the Wave Principle and therefore of social mood is the stock market. In socionomic terms we can say that the stock market is a sociometer. A sociometer is an indicator of the ups and downs, i.e. the trends of social mood. The science of applying sociometers to forecasting is termed sociometrics. Prechter suggests this term, which is why I shall be using it, too. However, I consider it a rather unfortunate term, as it seems to imply that we are dealing with a method that can provide us with certainty, just like Econometrics claims to do (but it is wrong in that case, too). But sociometrics, like Socionomics in general, deals with probabilities. It is important always to keep in mind that all forecasting and anticipation on the grounds of using sociometers is probabilistic.[233]

Sociometrics is applied Socionomics. It is the use of socionomic data and the application of sociometers to forecasting and anticipation. As such it can be used by administration's lookout staff for environmental monitoring, i. e. the monitoring of the basic crowd psychological waves of society, and for strategic planning during the preparatory work for new laws tackling future issues.

What ist important is that a sociometer can either help anticipate the tenor of future events or their character. Tenor relates to the negative or positive polar direction of a trend, whereas character refers to traits of social mood that we should expect while a trend unfolds. So, anticipating tenor merely makes a statement about the overall polar direction of a phenomenon. Forecasting character, however, is more specific and would state that we might have to expect people to be more ebullient and therefore more speculative in the financial markets for example, or that we have to be prepared to encounter more feelings of discord and therefore a higher degree of preparedness for racism.

Predictions of tenor are no doubt useful. They point us in the general direction that society might go. However, for legislative action, i. e. for the passing of laws it would be desirable to have information that is more specific. Possible anticipation of the character of future social actions and events is much more important here. Laws can hardly be made merely on the basis of the prediction that aggregate social mood will be rather negative during the next three years. Even very general laws need to have a subject, which they regulate.

Committees and administrative lookout staff will certainly find it most useful for their preparatory work to know something about the tenor of a trend since it can tell them on what kind of mood they will have to focus. But when it comes to the detailed formulation of a bill, most work will have to orient itself on the probable character of a trend.

Application

According to Prechter there are five points to keep in mind when applying sociometers to forecasting and anticipation:[234]

1. Leading sociometers predict the tenor and character of lagging ones. As certain actions take less time to execute than others, leading sociometers can tell us how other sociometers might develop and behave. For example, if we can observe a lot of optimism in the stock market as people invest we can predict a probable uptrend in the total investments made in the economy or the amount of money lending.
2. Lagging sociometers, if they are the only sociometric data available, can provide a basis for hypothesizing about the behavior of leading ones. Sometimes there are only lagging sociometers available or we are lacking data which would be necessary for a reliable statement about a leading sociometer. Lagging sociometers can then allow for conclusions to be drawn about leading ones and help fill the gaps in the information.
3. Lagging sociometers can sometimes help confirm presumed changes in leading ones. When a presumed change of trend has occurred in a leading sociometer, the behavior of a lagging one can help confirm or deny this assumption.
4. The extremes of a polar sociometer can help predict its changes. When a polar sociometer approaches one of its extremes, it is a strong sign that a change is about to occur. On lower or intermediate levels of recursion social mood does not get as close to the poles as on high levels of recursion. Therefore, it is easier to anticipate change and change is more probable to occur if the trend is on a high level of recursion. Progressive sociometers can help confirm assumptions of this kind due to the wave pattern they trace.
5. The Elliott wave patterns of a progressive sociometer can help predict its changes. Because progressive sociometers trace an Elliott wave pattern, with good knowledge of the Wave Principle it is possible to make predictions about changes in a progressive sociometer based purely on information supplied by that sociometer itself. This requires in-depth knowledge of the foundations of the Wave Principle as laid out in Part III. The pattern itself can tell us which way it is probably going to develop.

The last sentence should have made it clear once more: all forecasting and anticipation based on sociometers is probabilistic in nature. There can be no guarantee or certainty.

Data inexactness and impurity

No sociometer will give us a pure and exact measure of social mood. On the one hand, as we have already seen, a sociometer never measures mood itself but actions based on social mood. It might well be that some people do not act on their mood for whatever reason and therefore do not show up in the statistics. Others, however, might react extremely sensitively to the mood they are in, thereby not reflecting the average mood state.

Furthermore, the actions contributing to the data of a sociometer will not all be purely mood-induced. Some will have been taken for entirely different reasons – not the least of which will be logical thinking. A movie producer might decide to produce a movie, which in its character is contrary to his mood because it is cheaper to make and he gets more money from the film company. But as such actions will run both ways – positive and negative – they will more or less cancel each other out. The picture we get from a sociometer will not be perfect, but we can nonetheless expect it to reflect aggregate social mood quite well.

4.4.6 Focus – Operations Room

We have talked a lot about information gathering and the kind of information that is needed. However, all this information initially is mostly not information but data. It is a lot of figures and graphs and text – and no one knows what to do with it. These data need to be processed and brought into shape in such a way so the people who have to make decisions based on them understand them and can work with them. The data need to be transformed into information. For this we need what Stafford Beer calls a »Focus«. We need a place where all the various data are brought together and where they are condensed and visualized. We need a »decision platform«, something like a cockpit for organizations. Stafford Beer calls this an »Operations Room«.[235]

The Operations Room is an actual room that serves decision-makers as a cockpit or control center for whatever organization it is that they have to manage. Its beginnings go back to the early 1970s when Stafford Beer was a counselor to President Salvador Allende in Chile. Beer built the first prototype of the Operations Room in Santiago for the Chilean economy according to the considerations concerning System 4 made in his book *Brain of the Firm*.

Figure 43: Operations Room
Source: © Malik Management

As shown in Figure 44, three screens onto which the information about the system in question is projected constitute the heart of the Operations Room. The screen on the left is the Real-Time-Management-Information System.[236] It is the place where all the relevant strategic and operative figures are displayed. The real-time effect is achieved by certain statistical calculations, which are constantly run in the background. Newly incoming information is filtered and processed and alarm is sounded if significant deviations from the normal state occur. The screen in the middle is a model of the system itself. Here, the data is combined, which makes it possible to simulate different future scenarios that the system might have to face. The screen on the right contains the memory system. Earlier decisions and assumptions are saved there so they can be recalled upon demand at any later moment to see what has proven wrong and what was accurate.

The Operations room thus exhibits the four key elements of an effective decision platform:

1. A model of the system and its environment.
2. Real-time information.
3. A memory system.
4. The possibility to focus.

What the Operations Room provides is the possibility of continuous thinking about possible (and probable) »futures«. It has already been said above that planning is a continuous process. It is therefore the continued attention dedicated to the system and its changes which best assures that the right strategy is chosen. In our particular case, it is the continued thinking of parliamentary representatives about possible (and probable) developments of society, which alone guarantees better than anything else that the right laws are passed.

But reflection about the future is not yet enough. At some point a decision needs to be made and, as the name »decision platform« implies, the Operations Room is the place to make decisions. In our case, it would be the place where representatives can reach a decision on what laws need to be passed. As the behavior of a complex system such as society is foreseeable only to a certain extent even in socionomic terms, the reaching of a decision concerning a complex system must include:[237]

1. The ability to react to change in real time and based on relevant information.
2. The use of available knowledge and its integration in accurate models of the system.
3. Continued attention to the futures of the system and its environment and the anticipation and simulation of possible developments.
4. Systematic learning by following the decisions made and their assumptions and expectations.
5. Efficiency of the decision-making process by focusing on the relevant.

The framework provided by the Operations Room creates an environment which allows for the integration of these points into the decision-making process and thereby helps come to sound and good decisions.

As the term »Focus« implies, the Operations Room is where all information comes together and is focused. I imagine that there might well be several Operations Rooms for the different departments, agencies and committees in the legislature's administration. From there, already filtered information could run to a central Operations Room, which would serve representatives as the core decision platform.

Of course, decisions made in the Operations Room cannot replace the regular process that leads to the passing of a law. A bill must still be sent to the floor and pass the formal requirements. But prior to this the Operations Room might help come up with better drafts and sounder argumentation and prove valuable to legislative committees and even possible mediating commissions between chambers.

4.5 On the character of laws passed and legislative instruments

A central problem for any legislature dealing with future issues must be the character of laws that are being passed. This problem has two aspects. First, the question is how detailed a law should be. After all, as we have seen, such laws are merely dealing with probabilities within a very general context. Any anticipatory mechanism is unable to tell us anything about specific developments. Second, the question needs to be addressed of how and when laws come into effect or can be invalidated, i. e. what legislative instruments there are to help us handle the specific character of anticipatory laws. Again, the problem is that we are dealing with probabilities. If the legislative system is too rigid, it will not be able to adapt quickly to changes concerning the probabilities that actually fulfill themselves in the end.

4.5.1 General vs. detailed laws

An anticipatory mechanism allows us to foresee the future only in very general terms. As stated above, it can never help us guess what the specific shaping of things will be. That would be mere speculation and, except for Nostradamus, nobody has so far been able to tell what is coming (and it is more than doubtful whether Nostradamus' prophecies are not »correct« by virtue of our interpretation of them in retrospect). In any case, such speculation cannot be the basis for the passing of laws, as we might just as well roll the dice to see what is going to happen. Any law passed needs to be adjusted to the means available to us of peeking into the future. These means, i. e. Socionomics, provide us with a rather rough overview of the tenor and character of things to come. Therefore, laws made to regulate such future issues must naturally be rather »rough« as well.

This is also supported by cybernetics – as we have seen. Society is a complex system, and such systems cannot be controlled by detailed regulation. This would lead to the exact opposite, namely the loss of control over the system. Control must take place on a very general level only and, therefore, the law must have a regulative effect on this very general level only as well.

The most with which we can work, then, is pattern recognition. Consistent with the insights of complexity theory, Socionomics can help us anticipate the tenor and character of the future social environment by means of the observation of recognizable patterns. Thus, law which aims at the regulation of future issues and is based on socionomic insights needs to operate on the same level of abstraction. It is on this general level – and on this level only – that anticipatory law has its justification. Laws regulating the supposed details and specifics of developments and environments to come have no basis. This is a very important point. As there is a difference in terms of uncertainty between the big picture and the detailed shaping of the future in terms of the information with which Socionomics can provide us, we need to take this difference into consideration when legislating: It is possible to anticipate the general tenor and character of future developments, hence, laws can be made to apply to this. On the other hand, it is impossible to predict any details and therefore, it is impossible to make any laws which would apply to any such details.

This being said, there remains one question: Where should we draw the line between »sufficiently general« and »too detailed«? To answer this question we must think of what it is that we are trying to achieve. An anticipatory legislative mechanism is supposed to prepare society for future changes and developments before they occur, thereby avoiding legal gaps and preventing possible system breakdowns. New changes and developments should be able to unfold peacefully and smoothly within the existing order. For this to happen, there needs to be a channel or a framework which guarantees that the new develops in an orderly way alongside the old and does not threaten overall stability. This is what the law is supposed to provide: the channel, the framework – and nothing more.

The legal frame is there to make sure that a change of some sort will be compatible with existing structures or that there will at least be a smooth transition. By »existing structure«, I mean foremost the basic values and institutions of a society such as, for example, freedom, property, the rule of law, certain fundamental human rights, etc.[238] The questions guiding the legislative process in the face of a supposed development must therefore be of the following nature:

- What safeguards are really necessary for the peaceful protection of the fundamental values of society and which ones can be done without?
- What are the least drastic measures that can guarantee such protection?
- Are there any measures that infringe less on people's freedom than the ones so far proposed by at the same time still achieving the desired goal?
- What would be the most general law that can still achieve what we think necessary?
- What measures are necessary but also sufficient to achieve our goal?

These exemplary questions should make clear what I mentioned before: The law is there to provide a framework – and nothing more. Lawmakers should refrain strictly from passing laws which might result in regulation beyond absolute necessity. Since we can only make statements about the general character of trends and developments, laws should be kept as general as possible as well. Otherwise we would again run the risk of legislating based on mere speculation. In addition to that, change of any sort should be allowed to unfold freely as long as it does not threaten social order. The complex self-regulating mechanisms of society should be free to operate within a given framework. Again, things are far too complex for anyone to grasp, let alone control. So the details and specifics that will result from a particular development are something a legislature neither can nor should be influencing.

Trying to do so would be counterproductive, as it would sooner or later lead to a complete entanglement of the government with social life and, as a result, either to more and more authoritative structures or to a destructive loss of control over the system.

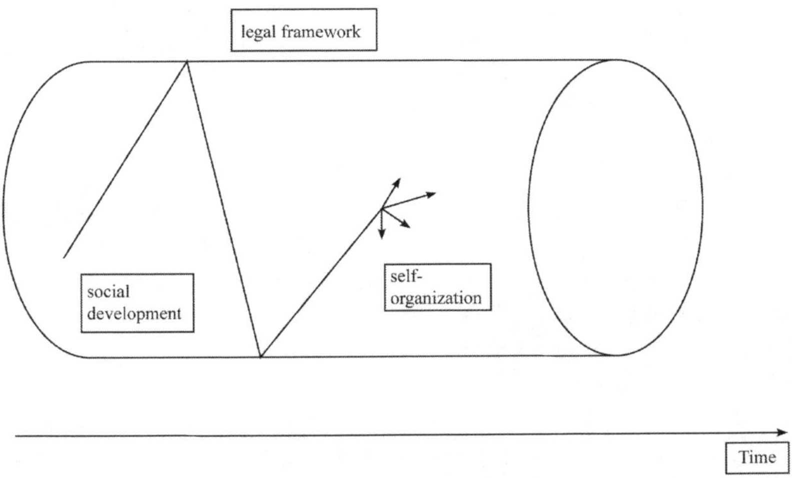

Figure 44: Legal framework and societal self-organization

As unsatisfying as it is, I do not believe that it is possible to come up with an exact statement about what kind of law should be considered acceptable in terms of its generality and what kind should be deemed too detailed. The decision depends on the issue concerned and on the question of how specific a statement can be made based on the socionomic data available. If all we can do is to say that the overall tenor of social mood will most likely be approaching a negative extreme in the next few years, then all lawmakers can do is to try provide the most basic and general safeguards. However, there will be cases when the data available allows for more specific statements about the character of a future mood trend and, based on experience, maybe even about probable manifestations of this trend. In these cases regulations, which are more detailed, could be considered acceptable. In the end, each case will have to be judged separately and it will to some degree depend on the experience and the judgment of the lawmakers how detailed a law should be. However, the goal must always be to come up with the least infringing regulation, with a regulation that is necessary but also sufficient.

4.5.2 Legislating for probabilities

An obvious problem is the question of how and when laws having the regulation of future issues as their subject should come into effect or rather should be invalidated and what instruments the legislature can use to address the special nature of such laws. We are dealing with probabilities. This means that we can never be certain that a supposed change or development will actually occur. And even if it occurs maybe its character will not be as anticipated.

Imagine, therefore, having passed a new law based on data derived from several sociometers. The work was thoroughly conducted; no mistakes were made – yet things happen differently. Maybe the period of time over which the trend develops is longer than expected and supposed negative effects take longer to manifest themselves. Or maybe the trend takes a significantly positive turn once more when an immediate negative development was expected. Without having the possibility in such a situation either to delay the coming into effect of a law, invalidate it or put it on hold for the time being, society could be stuck with a regulation that could prove to be harmful to its development and maybe even cause more damage than it would do good if circumstances had been as expected in the first place.

We are not dealing with present problems, which are there for everyone to see, and the only thing that needs to be done is to find the right solution for them (although even this might be beyond anyone's power). We are concerned with probable future problems and we cannot be certain if they will really occur. This is why legislation must be flexible when dealing with them. Because laws are made for things that are only probably going to happen, there must be ways to adjust the legislative process accordingly.

Even more than legislation as we know it now, legislation for future issues must be a continuous process. The social trends must constantly remain under observation. For this reason, it might be useful to have an administrative staff committee whose task would be the monitoring of anticipatory laws. It must be possible to adjust the law at any time if a trend unfolds differently than anticipated. Of course, this does not mean that adjustments can be random. They must always be based on socionomic data and new insights into the development of a trend, as some probabilities cease to apply and others appear.

What legislation therefore needs is a set of instruments to do this special situation justice and cope with it effectively and quickly.

Legal level

Regulations can be passed on different levels in terms of their legal hierarchy. Changes or amendments can be made to the constitution, which would be the highest level. The constitution contains the most fundamental values and principles of a society and all other legal regulations are derived from it. As a result of its importance, the possibility of constitutional alterations is often limited. Usually, there are particular majorities needed[239] such as two thirds of Congress and three quarters of the states in the United States[240] or two thirds of both the Bundestag and the Bundesrat in Germany.[241] As anticipatory regulations are supposed to make society adaptable to future influences, and as this means that one needs to be rather flexible in their handling, the constitution cannot be the right place for them. It must be possible to change them rather easily and without the kind of majority that one usually needs to change the constitution. Anticipatory regulations are not made to contain the fundamental values of society. They are there to protect them as they are written down in the constitution.

Therefore, anticipatory legislation must happen on levels below the constitution. This means that regulations must be passed either as formal laws or as decrees. In any case, in accordance with Hayek's constitutional model, the legislature must be responsible for the passing. In most countries this automatically means that it can only be formal laws that can contain such regulations and not decrees, as decrees are mostly lawmaking instruments of the executive. Switzerland is an exception in this respect because of the direct democratic factor of the political system, but even here parliament's possibilities for passing regulations as decrees are extremely limited.

Formal laws derive their validity from the constitution and must not violate it. But they are easier to pass and change in terms of the majority needed. This means more flexibility in the handling of matters. Still, there is a rigid formal procedure prior to the passing of a bill. On the one hand, this procedure constitutes a structural safeguard against arbitrariness and supports the decision-making process. On the other hand, it makes legislation slow and restricts the flexibility that might be needed in anticipatory matters. Here, decrees passed by the executive could help. This would, of course, violate the constitutional model suggested here, but I would not rule out the possibility completely. In a very limited scope and related to well-defined matters, executive decrees could support the flexible handling of anticipatory regulations. In general, however, this flexibility needs to be found in the legislative instruments that a legislative assembly has when passing a bill.

Legislative instruments[242]

Different scenarios

We are faced with probabilities and, therefore, there are not just one but various possible scenarios. One way of coping with the variety created by this fact is to come up with various drafts of a law in advance. Such drafts would have to orient themselves on different probable trend developments, so that whatever scenario comes true there is a draft that applies and can be sent to the floor to be passed. A similar approach has been suggested under the name of »regulations ›in stock‹«.[243]

It is clear that it is not possible to come up with drafts for all possible scenarios. However, it might well be that it is possible to come up with drafts for all probable scenarios or at least for many of them. Remember that we are trying to find regulative solutions on a rather general and abstract level, on the level of patterns only. Translated into socionomic terms this means that we are also dealing with rather high levels of recursion in terms of the unfolding of the Elliot Wave pattern. High levels of recursion correspond to long periods of time, so there is enough time to prepare for the corresponding waves. Also, Prechter has found it easier to apply the Wave Principle to waves of higher levels of recursion, as we can be more certain about the development of the big picture than about the unfolding of smaller waves over the next few weeks: »In fact, contrary to all current views on the subject, it is the long-term social trends, the ones that chaos scientists say are impossible to predict, that are in fact easier to predict.«[244]

Anticipatory legislation should not be dealing with short-term developments anyway. It would otherwise again fall into the trap of taking on details and that is not its task.

Conditional laws

Another feasible way of handling probabilities would be to attach certain conditions to a law. Conditions are an instrument well known to and widely used in contract law where »a condition is given if the binding character or the dissolution of a contract depends on an uncertain fact«.[245] In legal terms the former is called a »condition precedent« and the latter a »condition subsequent«. Legislation could make use of this instrument in the same way as contract law.

Condition precedent: One or several conditions are attached to a law in order for it to come into force. In case one or some of them are not fulfilled, the law remains inoperative. For example, a condition for a law to come into force could be for the Wave pattern of a particular level of recursion in the Dow Jones Industrial Average to break, let us say, the point barrier of 8000 points, as this would indicate and support a particular continuation of the pattern. Many hitherto probable developments could be disregarded and others would become more likely.

Condition subsequent: A law is passed which remains in force as long as certain conditions are not fulfilled. The law just mentioned could, for example, remain in effect as long as the DJIA does not break 8250 points, as this would indicate a reversal of the trend in which case the law would no longer be applicable.

From a legal point of view, there are certain problems with applying conditions to legislation.[246] They would have to be applied with great care in any case. However, conditions could prove to be a useful instrument for anticipatory legislative action. On the one hand, they could set limits to the arbitrariness of lawmakers. Laws could not simply be invalidated or made effective according to representatives' liking, but would instead be governed by agreed conditions based on socionomic facts. On the other hand, conditions could be effective safeguards against the probabilities of trend development and human mistakes. Be it that a trend develops differently or that mistakes were made during preparatory work, conditions could operate as a safety net and help to avoid greater damage.

Time limit

A less flexible way than conditions would be to set a definite time limit to the coming into effect or the invalidation of a law. If the turning point of a trend could be more or less anticipated, then the validity of a law could be limited in advance, so as to avoid any harmful effects due to the longevity of a no longer useful law.

A combination of time limits and conditions would also be imaginable. One could, for example, pass a law which would only come into effect if certain sociometers behave in a particular way (condition). However, after a certain period of time the law would expire if the condition had not been fulfilled by then. Thus, the degree of uncertainty as to what will happen legally could be diminished.

Although anticipatory laws need to be monitored constantly, a time limit to the validity of a law would force the legislature even more to keep an eye on it. It would foster the understanding of legislation as a continuous process and make sure laws are either renewed on time or replaced by more appropriate ones.[247]

Legislation by means of limited regulations in terms of time is sometimes also termed »experimental lawmaking« and seems to be of ever-greater importance. The reason is that, with complex matters and changing circumstances, it is difficult to tell if a law will have the desired effect.[248] The same is true in our case, since we are dealing with probabilities. It is therefore necessary to monitor a law and compare expectations and actual effect, so as to be ready if action needs to be taken because things take an unexpected turn.

Transitional arrangements[249]

In case of drastic measures and therefore drastic changes to the law, it might be wise to pass some sort of transitional regulation. Such arrangements could directly be contained in a new law or be passed as separate laws ahead of the actual law. Interim regulations would serve to help people adapt to new legal situations and avoid hardship. This could be achieved by temporal measures, such as limitations or the time of coming into force of regulations, or measures such as the option to choose between the old and the new law for a certain period of time.

Transitional arrangements would not address the probability character of anticipatory laws directly. But they could be used as a possibly less harmful »try-out phase«. Transitional laws could be passed as a weaker preliminary state. On the one hand, such laws would communicate necessary signals about what will have to be expected in the future and pre-guide social behavior. On the other hand, in case the supposed development does not occur, they would not be as harmful and could be invalidated more easily.

Emergency laws

The concept of laws being put into effect without the usually necessary proceedings is nothing new in cases of emergency.[250] Most parliamentary systems have it. What would be new about an anticipatory emergency law is that the emergency would have been foreseen and the law would already have been waiting. The only unknown would be the exact time the emergency happens. This would, at least, be the ideal case. Of course, the hope would be not to have an emergency in the first place thanks to the anticipatory mechanism of the legislature. But as social mood is endogenous, some extreme manifestations might not be entirely avoidable. So although certain emergencies might occur, they would occur with all or at least most of the necessary measures waiting and with the authorities prepared.

4.6 Possible jurisprudential obstacles to anticipatory legislation

There are certain principles that pervade the legal sciences. They have evolved in a long process in which the courts have often played a key role and constitute some of the most reliable pillars of the law. Many have found their way into our modern constitutions and together with the fundamental human rights they exist in order to restrict government action and protect the freedom of the individual.

Because of this, I consider it worth having a quick look at the issue of anticipatory legislation from the point of view of these principles, as there are certain questions as to their compatibility.

4.6.1 Legal certainty

The most prominent question is probably whether anticipatory legislation can be compatible with the principle of legal certainty. Legal certainty protects »the confidence of the individual citizen in the foreseeability, predictability and consistency of the law«.[251] The citizens must be able to rely on some continuity. They must be able to put their trust in the fact that a legislative assembly does not alter the law without difficulty. Rehbinder breaks it down into the two concepts of »certainty and practicability« and says that in order for the law to guarantee these two things it needs to stick to what is recognizable and provable.[252]

If you look at the subject of anticipatory law, which consists of probabilities, then there seems to be a clear violation of the principle of legal certainty as there is nothing provable. In addition to that, the flexibility needed to cope with the changing variety created by those probabilities seems incompatible with the demand for foreseeability, predictability and consistency. However, this is so only at first glance.

When talking about the concept of provability, we need to distinguish between lawmaking, i. e. legislation, and the application of law by the courts. In legislation there is no room for it. All normative laws can by definition not be proven. Of course, law must not be arbitrary.[253] The sources to which the legislation relates should be accurate, the information correct, but we cannot say that the law needs to be provable. Where proof plays a decisive role is in the application of law by the courts and the executive. It is there that the facts count when having to decide whether a law applies to a particular case or not.

A more serious problem is posed by the flexibility in handling the law to cope with probabilities, as I have been suggesting. A continuous adaptation and alteration of a draft or the existence of several drafts is of course not a problem yet. Already today, we cannot expect our representatives to tell us in advance what kind of law they are going to pass. Foreseeability, predictability and consistency, which the principle of legal certainty demands, come in once a law has been passed and is in force. It is from this moment on that the individual citizen has a right to a certain security against unnecessary alterations and to some consistency. The concept of conditional laws, in particular, could indeed pose a threat to this, as could time limits and transitional arrangements used as interim phases.

I believe, however, that it depends on the way in which conditions – and indeed any other legislative instruments – are used. It is clear that they should be used with care. They should be used only where they are believed to be really necessary and where their absence could mean that a law which has become harmful for society remains in force (or, in the opposite case, that a necessary law would not come into effect). I would suggest that conditions and time limits be specifically marked upon publication of the law. Such a measure would guarantee that people are informed about the special character of a law and can adjust their behavior accordingly.

Furthermore, I think that there should be limits in terms of the time span for which a conditional law should be valid. This has already been mentioned. It would be a combination of conditional laws with time limits. It is untenable with the principle of legal certainty that a law be passed, then does not come into effect because the conditions are not fulfilled, but is subsequently kept alive for ten or more years. This kind of uncertainty would be unreasonable for anyone.

Other than that, I do not see any greater problems or conflicts with the principle of legal certainty. It is clear that it is important to inform the public about anticipatory laws. But this is a matter of course. Laws must to be published before they can come into effect. Maybe anticipatory laws should be marked specially and conditions and time limits should be highlighted. And maybe even possible alternative drafts should be published as well. But as long as good public information is guaranteed and no laws are passed beyond what is believed to be necessary, I believe that even flexible handling and possible continuous alterations to the law do not have to violate the principle of legal certainty.

4.6.2 Prohibition of arbitrary decision-making[254]

We are dealing with probabilities. So we do not really know what is going to happen. Still we pass laws for possible and probable scenarios. But at the same time we want to remain flexible enough to alter or invalidate the law in case we are mistaken and the supposed development does not occur. This might seem somewhat arbitrary: »We think that this and that is going to happen. So let's pass a law and if it doesn't fit we can always change it.« It is not like that of course.

According to the principle of prohibition of arbitrary decision-making, a law constitutes a violation of the principle »if it cannot be based on serious and objective reasons«.[255] Socionomic data is serious and objective. Just because Socionomics gives us probabilities to work with and not certainties, it does not mean that decisions based on it are random and not objective. As long as the basis of a new law is the information that can be gained by socionomic means, there are objective reasons on which the law is founded. A legislative assembly passing laws based on such information cannot be accused of arbitrary legislation.

The principles of legal certainty and of the prohibition of arbitrary decision-making need to be taken seriously when talking about an anticipatory mechanism for legislation. If set up the wrong way, such a mechanism could indeed violate these principles, especially that of legal certainty. But I believe that there are ways of instituting it in conformity with these principles. We have long experience with the problems and difficulties that can arise in connection with them. There are countless court rulings and cases that can guide us in dealing with these matters. I believe that this experience is just as applicable to anticipatory law as it is to the law that we have today and that there is no need to look for solutions other than the ones that we already have.

Of course, there are many other principles guiding the legal sciences in addition to legal certainty and the prohibition of arbitrary decision-making such as the rule of law, equality before the law or exclusion of retroactive effects. I do not see in which way anticipatory laws might threaten them, however. Anticipatory legislation does not turn the legal sciences upside down. It simply broadens the scope of legislative action while remaining subject to the same principles that guide the law today.

5. Further afield

5.1 Federalism

I believe that a direct implication of what has been said is that the best way to organize a country is federalism. Not that it is not possible to have a centralized organization in a nation. But for a couple of reasons that have been mentioned I believe federalism to be the optimal choice.

First, the Viable System Model states that the Systems 1 have to be viable systems themselves. Applied to countries this means that member states, be they provinces, »Kantone«, states or »Bundesländer«, are Systems 1 with complete autonomy, except where the cohesion of the entire country is threatened. In a centralized state this is extremely difficult to achieve. There would constantly be the risk of overloading the central command line running from the meta-system to System 1, thereby depriving the latter of its autonomy and rendering impossible an optimal absorption of variety. In my opinion, centralization – or at least rigid centralization, as certain aspects of centralization are absolutely necessary – is incompatible with the structure of the Viable System. Only federalism can effectively cope with the member states as autonomous Systems 1 because (at least partial) autonomy is already part of the understanding of federalism. This autonomy given to the member states leads at least to the possibility of optimal variety absorption, as this can only happen on the member state level. A central authority does not have requisite variety to absorb the variety generated on the lower level and Ashby's law would assert itself in a way that would be harmful to society.

Second, because of the complexity of society as a system and because of the rather general outlook Socionomics can grant us, the nature of laws passed should be as general as possible. Now, if a country were organized in a federal way, i. e. divided into member states which are given more or less autonomy in their own dealings, such as Switzerland, the United States or Canada, this principle would still lead to more detailed laws than in a centralized country – but in a good way. If a member state needs to absorb the variety generated on its level itself then this means that it must be allowed to pass law applicable to its own matters. Clearly, a member state has much more information about what is happening on its territory than a federal government could ever have. Hence, even very general laws on member state level would be more specific than on the federal level and would absorb much more variety than federal laws applicable to state matters ever could. And the same is true if we go down to the community level. This way, a lot more variety could be absorbed overall than it could if there were only one central authority whose concern needs to be matters of all three levels.

I am not saying that it is impossible to organize a country in a centralized way. After all, many countries are centralized and have been so throughout their entire history. But I believe that such countries are not as robust and are structurally more vulnerable. Centralization leads to a larger governmental apparatus, less understanding of the problems of the citizens, and less flexibility and adaptability. In a federal state the federal government is much better able to focus on problems that concern the cohesion and the viability of the entire country, as problems are solved at the level where they can be solved best.

5.2 Social mood and representatives

Waves of social mood diffuse all social aggregates. Legislative assemblies are no exception. Just like other people, representatives are subject to fluctuations in social mood, and just like other people, they are more or less likely to act on their current sentiment. We would like to think that people are elected as representatives who are more objective and more open-minded – people who rise above the crowd – and that, because of this, they are less prone to succumb to their impulsive moods. But this is, of course, not so. In a democracy – and especially in the kind of democracy that is common today – people are elected that are no different from you and me. So they, too, are influenced by social mood.

The danger, therefore, is that representatives make laws in accordance with their mood. We saw an example of this in Part I when we looked at stock market and financial legislation in the United States in the twentieth century. What happens, then, is that legislatures swim along with the current and by doing so do quite the opposite of what it is that they are supposed to do – to operate as a force neutralizing destructive trends in society and act as an institution of guidance for the long-term sake of society.

There is one more problem. Not only are the members of a legislative assembly subject to social mood. At times, they can also show characteristics of advanced crowds. Le Bon saw this clearly and dedicated a whole chapter in his book to parliamentary assemblies. I do not think that all his comments are correct. But especially when it comes to party factions in legislative assemblies the unity of mind can be tremendous. Members of a faction can be so biased as to their own party line that they are unable to discuss arguments of another party reasonably. And looking at the behavior of representatives, it is difficult to deny that they are sometimes closer to the behavioral level of a twelve year-old than that of a grown-up.

Still, many features of advanced crowds are missing in parliamentary bodies. There can be no critical mass and no discharge, as a legislative »crowd« naturally cannot grow. Maybe we could say that what can be observed in legislative bodies is a mixture of crowd characteristics and group characteristics. We did not deal with the particular characteristics of groups and we cannot go into the details here. But there is research dedicated especially to groups suggesting that groups can induce a special kind of behavior in people.[256] This behavior can be similar to the behavior people show in a crowd, but it does not necessarily need to be the same. However, just like crowds, groups are able to produce their own social realities.[257] Studies suggest that groups tend to »convince themselves«. Even very intelligent people can come to completely wrong conclusions on perfectly rational matters due to the dynamics of the group. »Belonging to the same group tends to produce changes in opinions and attitudes in the direction of establishing uniformity within the group.«[258] In parliamentary parties this seems to happen quite often.

Fortunately, representatives do not always behave that way and are often very well able to preserve their individual capabilities.

»Fortunately all the characteristics just described as to be met with in parliamentary assemblies are in no wise constantly displayed. Such assemblies only constitute crowds at certain moments. The individuals composing them retain their individuality in a great number of cases, which explains how it is that an assembly is able to turn out excellent technical laws«.[259]

Still, representatives are human beings – not machines – so there is no guarantee that they will not act based on their emotions, their mood or crowd tendency. In Part III, we saw how powerful the limbic system can be. That is the reason why our institutions need to be designed in a way that will mitigate human weaknesses and defaults. Part of this design is the expert staff, which makes sure the relevant information is collected and made known to representatives. As Le Bon puts it: »It is specialists who safeguard assemblies from passing ill-advised or unworkable measures.«[260] Part of this design is also the Operations Room, which offers the best possible environment for decision-making based on objective information.

In the end, of course, it is still people who decide. No matter how good a system is, it can never be perfect as long as human beings are involved. I believe, however, that a system which contains the elements listed here would have good chances of achieving what it has been set up to do. Social mood will still be part of every representative's personality, but the design of the system would make sure that it would not be part of the laws passed.

6. Conclusions and outlook

As utopian as an anticipatory mechanism for our legislatures might seem, the problem that led me to propose it is very real. The law lags behind societal changes and developments. This fact can, at times, bring about situations that are harmful or even disastrous to a society, as in the case of revolutions, wars and manias in the financial markets. As long as we do not find ways to »break the time barrier«[261] and anticipate society's path in the future, such events are bound to recur time and again. They will find governments as unprepared as ever with nothing left but the attempt to put back together the pieces after things have fallen apart.

Managerial cybernetics and crowd psychological studies point us in the right direction for tackling the problem. Managerial cybernetics helps to understand how control in complex systems works and how a system needs to be designed and organized in order to be able to anticipate and cope with future developments. Crowd psychology fosters the understanding of one of the fundamental mechanisms and driving forces of society. The new science of Socionomics, then, can help us use this mechanism for the anticipation of society's future course. If we merge all the insights that we can gain from these disciplines we are – for the first time – able to redesign our lawmaking bodies in a way which will enable them to act in genuine anticipation and preparation of future developments instead of simply reacting to them.

Crowd psychological phenomena are the source of fundamental social change. As advanced crowds cannot be controlled, our focus needs to be on basic crowds. Their development has to be channeled and mitigated so they do not give birth to advanced crowds and the change that they potentially bring with them does not threaten social peace and order. This means that law has to be made prior to such developments. Stafford Beer's Viable System Model and the use of the socionomic approach within System 4 open up the view for the future. They provide the means for setting up an anticipatory legislative mechanism. Equipped with such a mechanism the legislature would be able to pass law applicable to future crowd psychological social changes, thus preparing society for tomorrow.

The way to an anticipatory legislative mechanism, though, is full of obstacles. Today, both the dependence of our legislative bodies on interest groups and their shortsightedness are immanent parts of our republican systems. Before there can be any real talk of legislatures performing an anticipatory function, these problems need solving. Moreover, science is only just starting to realize what benefit crowd psychological research can have for the explanation of human behavior; Socionomics is still a young theory that remains a work in progress as it becomes refined, and cybernetic approaches are still far from being common knowledge. This means that we are only at the beginning of the understanding of these new approaches and of what might well lead to a revolution in the social sciences.

The ideas introduced here constitute but a rough outline. Much more work will be necessary to elaborate and sophisticate them for practical use – the System-4 function needs to be implemented in detail, the crowd and its mechanisms need to be studied more thoroughly, and suitable sociometers need to be found and developed, to name but a few necessary future projects. And it will certainly be some time still before there are people ready to give them a chance. But it is my conviction that we have to start now – and that we can.

What is certain, however, is that our standard approaches do not suffice to bring about such a mechanism. We need to change our way of thinking if we want to overcome the problems that our current system regularly encounters. I think that the direction is given. Time will tell if we will be able to make use of the new possibilities with which managerial cybernetics, crowd psychology and Socionomics provide us. If we fail, history is certain to repeat itself.

As Max Planck once said: »A new scientific truth does not triumph by convincing its opponents and making them see the light, but rather because its opponents eventually die, and a new generation grows up that is familiar with it.«[262]

Literature

Archiv für Rechts- und Sozialphilosophie (ARSP): *Globalisierung als Problem von Gerechtigkeit und Steuerungsfähigkeit des Rechts.* Stuttgart 2001

Archiv für Rechts- und Sozialphilosophie (ARSP): *Herausforderungen an das Recht am Ende des 20. Jahrhunderts*. Stuttgart 1995.

Archiv für Rechts- und Sozialphilosophie (ARSP): *Law and the Future of Society.* Wiesbaden 1979.

Arthur, W. Brian: »Inductive Reasoning and Bounded Rationality (The El Farol Problem)«, in: *American Economic Review* (Papers and Proceedings). Vol. 84,406, 1994.

Ashby, Ross: *An introduction to cybernetics.* London 1964.

Basedow, Jürgen/Kono, Toshiyuki (Eds.): *Legal Aspects of Globalization.* The Hague 2000.

Beer, Stafford: *Brain of the Firm.* Chichester 1994 (quotes: Beer, Brain).

Beer, Stafford: *Decision and Control.* Chichester 1994 (quotes: Beer, Decision).

Beer, Stafford: *The Heart of Enterprise.* Chichester 1994 (quotes: Beer, Heart).

Böckel, Markus: *Instrumente der Einpassung neuen Rechts in die Rechtsordnung.* Berlin 1993.

Bombach, Gottfried. »Lange Wellen«, in: Borner, S./Meyer,W. *Was Meint der Ökonom dazu?* Basel 1979.

Bonabeau, Eric/Meyer, Christopher: »Swarm Intelligence: A Whole New Way to Think About Business«, in: *Harvard Business Review,* May 2001.

Bühl, Walter L.: *Sozialer Wandel im Ungleichgewicht.* Stuttgart 1990.

Caflisch, Luciu: »The Role of Law and of Legal Science in the next Century«, in: *Keio Law Review*, Tokyo 1993.

Canetti, Elias: *Crowds and Power.* New York 1973.

Dewey, Edward R./Dakin, Edwin F.. Cycles: *The Science of Prediction.* 5th Ed. New York 1947.

Drucker, Peter: *The Frontiers of Management: Where Tomorrow's Decisions are Being Shaped Today.* New York 1986 (quotes: Drucker, Frontiers).

Drucker, Peter: *The New Realities.* London 1989.

Druey, Jean Nicolas: »Der juristische Lehrplan im Jahre 2050«, in: Meier-Schatz, Christian J.: *Die Zukunft des Rechts.* Basel 1999.

Ebke, Werner F.. »Die Zukunft der Rechtsetzung in multijurisdiktionalen Rechtsordnungen. Wettbewerb der Rechtsordnungen oder zentrale Regelvorgabe – am

Beispiel des Gesellschafts- und Unternehmensrechts«, in: Meier-Schatz, Christian J.: *Die Zukunft des Rechts.* Basel 1999.

Festinger, Leon: »Informal Social Communication«, in: *Psychological Review*, Vol 57 1950, p. 271–282.

Festinger, Leon/Thibaut, John: »Interpersonal Communication in small groups«, in: *Journal of abnormal social Psychology*, Vol. 46 1951, p. 92–99

Freud, Sigmund: *Massenpsychologie und Ich-Analyse.* 6th Edition. Frankfurt 2002.

Frost, Alfred J./Prechter, Robert, R.: *Elliott Wave Principle.* Gainsville 1998.

Gauch, Peter/Schluep, Walter R./Schmid, Jörg/Rey, Heinz: *Schweizerisches Obligationenrecht Allgemeiner Teil.* Vol. II, 8th Edition, Zürich 2003 (quotes: Gauch et al.).

Gerster, Hans Joachim: *Lange Wellen wirtschaftlicher Entwicklung: empirische Analyse langfristiger Zyklen für die USA, Großbritannien und weitere vierzehn Industrieländer von 1800 bis 1980.* Frankfurt 1988.

Gladwell, Malcolm: *The Tipping Point.* Boston 2000.

Häfelin, Ulrich/Haller, Walter: *Schweizerisches Bundesstaatsrecht.* 6th Edition. Zürich 2005.

Häfelin, Ulrich/Müller, Georg: *Allgemeines Verwaltungsrecht.* 4th Edition. Zürich 2002.

Hayek, Friedrich A. v.: *Law, Legislation and Liberty.* Volume I. Chicago and London 1973 (quotes: Hayek, Liberty, Vol. I).

Hayek, Friedrich A. v.: Law, *Legislation and Liberty.* Volume III. Chicago and London 1979 (quotes: Hayek, Liberty, Vol. III).

Hayek, Friedrich A. v.: *Die Theorie komplexer Phänomen*e. Tübingen 1972.

Hetzler, Sebastian: »Die Architektur richtiger Entscheidungen«, in: *Online Blatt*, Malik Management Zentrum St. Gallen, August 2005.

Janis, Irving Lester: *Groupthink: psychological studies of policy decisions and fiascoes.* 2nd Edition. Boston 1982.

Kirchgässner, Gebhard: *Homo Oeconomicus.* 2nd Edition. Tübingen 2000.

Kloepfer, Michael: »Zukunft und Recht«, in: *Das Recht in Raum und Zeit – Festschrift für Martin Lendi.* Zürich 1998.

Kramer, Ernst: »Konvergenz und Internationalisierung der juristischen Methode«, in: Meier-Schatz, Christian J.: *Die Zukunft des Rechts.* Basel 1999.

Le Bon, Gustave: *Psychologie des foules.* 7th Edition. Paris 2002.

Le Bon, Gustave: *The Crowd: A Study of the Popular Mind.* 1896. Kitchener, Ont. 2001

Lendi, Martin: *In die Zeit gesprochen – Reflexionen zu Recht und Politik.* Zürich 1990.

Leonard, Allenna: *Between momentum and control: a dynamic of democracy.* 2005 (unpublished paper).

Livas, Javier: *The Cybernetic State.* Mexico City 2003.

Livingstone, Stephen/Morison, John. Law, Society and Change. Dartmouth 1990.

Mager, Nathan H.: *The Kondratieff Waves.* New York 1987.

Malik, Fredmund: *Strategie des Managements Komplexer Systeme.* 8th Edition. Bern, Stuttgart and Wien 2003 (quotes: Malik, Strategie).

Malik, Fredmund: *Management. Das A und O des Handwerks.* Frankfurt 2005 (quotes: Malik, Management).

Marchetti, Cesare: »Society as a Learning System: Discovery, Invention, and Innovation Cycles Revisited«, in: *Syracuse Scholar.* Vol. 3 (2), 1982.

Marchetti, Cesare: »Stable Rules in Social and Economic Behavior«, in: *Bollettino degli Ingegneri* . Vol. XXXVI (6), 1988.

McDougall, William: *The Group Mind: A Sketch of the Principles of Collective Psychology with Some Attempt to Apply Them to the Interpretation of National Life and Character.* New York 1920.

Morison, John: »How to change things with rules«, in: Livingstone, Steven/Morison, John: *Law, Society and Change.* Dartmouth 1990.

Müller, Georg: *Elemente einer Rechtsetzungslehre.* Zürich 1999.

Neue Zürcher Zeitung am Sonntag. 9th October 2005.

Nobel Foundation, http://nobelprize.org.

Nofsinger, John/Kim, Kenneth: »Protecting Investors (not)«, in: Prechter Robert R.: *Pioneering Studies in Socionomics.* Gainsville 2003.

Ortega y Gasset, José: *Der Aufstand der Massen.* Stuttgart and München 2002.

Pelzmann, Linda: *M.o.M. Malik on Management.* November 2002 (quotes: Pelzmann, M.o.M.).

Pelzmann, Linda: *Wirtschaftspsychologie.* 3rd Edition. Wien 2000 (quotes: Pelzmann, Wirtschaftspsychologie).

Pelzmann, Linda/Malik, Constantin/Miklautz, Michaela: »The critical mass of preferences for customization«, in: Blecker, Thorsten/Friedrich, Gerhard (Eds.): *Mass Customization: Concepts, Tools, Realization.* Berlin 2005 (quotes: Pelzmann et al.).

Perez, Carlota: »Neue Technologien und sozio-institutioneller Wandel«, in: Thomas, H./Nefiodow, L.A.: *Kondratieffs Zyklen der Wirtschaft: An der Schwelle neuer Vollbeschaeftigung?* Herford 1998.

Perez, Carlota: »The Thought Leader Interview«, in: *Strategy and Business.* Issue 41, Winter 2005.

Popper, Karl: *Eine Welt der Propensitäten.* Tübingen 1995.

Posner, Richard A.: *Economic Analysis of Law.* 4th Edition. Boston 1992.

Prechter, Robert R.: *The Wave Principle of Human Social Behavior and the New Science of Socionomics.* Gainsville 1999 (quotes: Prechter, Wave Principle).

Prechter, Robert R.: *Pioneering Studies in Socionomics.* Gainsville 2003 (quotes: Prechter, Studies).

Rehbinder, Manfred: *Einführung in die Rechtswissenschaft.* 8th Edition. Berlin 1995.

Reich, Wilhelm: *Die Massenpsychologie des Faschismus.* Köln 1970.

Riesman, David: *The Lonely Crowd.* New Haven 1961.

Schäfer, Hans-Bernd/Ott, Claus: *Lehrbuch der ökonomischen Analyse des Zivilrechts.* 4th Edition. Berlin 2005.

Scheyhing, Robert: »Recht und Fortschrittsvorstellungen«, in: Gernhuber, Joachim: *Tradition und Fortschritt im Recht.* Tübingen 1977.

Schumpeter, J. A.: *Business Cycles.* New York and London 1939.

Schumpeter, J. A.: *Essays*. 6th Ed. New Brunswick 2003.
Shiller, Robert J.: »The Mystery of Economic Recessions«, in: *The New York Times*, 04.02.2001.
Solomou, Solomos: *Phases of Economic Growth, 1850 – 1973: Kondratieff Waves and Kuznets Swings*. 2nd Ed. Cambridge 1989.
Sunstein, Cass R.: *Behavioral Law and Economics*. Cambridge 2000.
Tarnas, Richard: *Idee und Leidenschaft. Die Wege des westlichen Denkens*. München 1997.
The Economist. 14.05.2005.
The Elliott Wave Theorist. September 2004 issue.
Thomas, Hans: »Zur Einführung«, in: Thomas, H./Nefiodow, L. A.: *Kondratieffs Zyklen der Wirtschaft. An der Schwelle neuer Vollbeschaeftigung?* Herford 1998.
Tversky, Amos/Kahneman, Daniel: »Rational Choice and the Framing of Decisions«, in: Kahneman, Daniel/Tversky, Amos (Eds.): *Choices, Values, and Frames*. Cambridge 2000.
Ziembinski, Zygmunt: »Future forms of steering society by means of law«, in: *Archiv für Rechts- und Sozialphilosophie. Law and the Future of Society*. Wiesbaden 1979.
Zippelius, Reinhold: *Rechtsphilosophie*. 3rd Edition. München 1994.

Legal sources

Bundesverfassung der Schweizerischen Eidgenossenschaft.
Constitution of the United States.
Grundgesetz für die Bundesrepublik Deutschland.

Notes

1 Morison, John: »How to change things with rules«, in: Livingstone, Steven/Morison, John: *Law, Society and Change.* Dartmouth 1990, 6.

2 Müller, Georg: *Elemente einer Rechtsetzungslehre.* Zürich 1999, p. 12 f. (Translation by C. Malik.)

3 Scheyhing, Robert: »Recht und Fortschrittsvorstellungen«, in: Gernhuber, Joachim: *Tradition und Fortschritt im Recht.* Tübingen 1977, p. 12 f. (Translation by C. Malik.)

4 See Posner, Richard A..: *Economic Analysis of Law.* Boston 1992; Schäfer, Hans-Bernd/Ott, Claus. *Lehrbuch der ökonomischen Analyse des Zivilrechts, 4. Auflage.* Berlin 2005.

5 Ebke, Werner F.: »Die Zukunft der Rechtsetzung in multijurisdiktionalen Rechtsordnungen. Wettbewerb der Rechtsordnungen oder zentrale Regelvorgabe – am Beispiel des Gesellschafts- und Unternehmensrechts«, in: Meier-Schatz, Christian J.: *Die Zukunft des Rechts.* Basel 1999, p. 106 ff.

6 Kramer, Ernst: »Konvergenz und Internationalisierung der juristischen Methode«, in: Meier-Schatz, Christian J.: *Die Zukunft des Rechts.* Basel 1999, p. 71.

7 Ziembinski, Zygmunt: »Future forms of steering society by means of law«, in: *Archiv für Rechts- und Sozialphilosophie. Law and the Future of Society.* Wiesbaden 1979, p. 43ff; Morison, p. 5ff; Müller, p. 11 ff.

8 Druey, Jean Nicolas: »Der juristische Lehrplan im Jahre 2050«, in: Meier-Schatz, Christian J.: *Die Zukunft des Rechts.* Basel 1999, p. 227; Caflisch, Luciu. »The Role of Law and of Legal Science in the next Century«, in: *Keio Law Review*, Tokyo 1993., p. 1ff; Basedow, Jürgen/Kono, Toshiyuki (Eds.): *Legal Aspects of Globalization.* The Hague 2000.

9 Müller, p. 12.

10 Shiller, Robert J.: »The Mystery of Economic Recessions«, in: *The New York Times*, February 4, 2001.

11 Prechter, Robert R.: *The Wave Principle of Human Social Behavior and the New Science of Socionomics.* Gainsville 1999, p. 371 f.

12 Livingstone, Stephen/Morison, John: *Law, Society and Change.* Dartmouth 1990; ARSP. *Herausforderungen an das Recht am Ende des 20. Jahrhunderts.* Stuttgart 1995; ARSP. *Globalisierung als Problem von Gerechtigkeit und Steuerungsfähigkeit des Rechts.* Stuttgart 2001; ARSP. *Law and the Future of Society.* Wiesbaden 1979; Basedow/Kono: *Legal Aspects of Globalization.*

13 *Neue Zürcher Zeitung am Sonntag*, 9.10.2005, p. 21. (Translation by C. Malik)
14 Nofsinger, John/Kim, Kenneth: »Protecting Investors (not)«, in: Prechter Robert R.. *Pioneering Studies in Socionomics*. Gainsville 2003.
15 Nofsinger/Kim, p. 223.
16 Marchetti, Cesare: »Society as a Learning System: Discovery, Invention, and Innovation Cycles Revisited«, in: *Syracuse Scholar*. Vol. 3 (2), 1982.; Marchetti, Cesare: »Stable Rules in Social and Economic Behavior«, in: *Bollettino degli Ingegneri* . Vol. XXXVI (6), 1988.
17 For more details on the term *mood* and the ramifications of this concept, see Part III Chapter 2.2.1.
18 See Part III Chapter 2. Socionomics – the science of social prediction.
19 Prechter, *Wave Principle*, p. 238.
20 See Part III Crowd Psychology and Socionomics.
21 Gladwell, Malcolm: *The Tipping Point*. Boston 2000.
22 Beer, Stafford: *The Heart of Enterprise*. Chichester 1994, p. 406.
23 Ashby, Ross: *An introduction to cybernetics*. London 1964, p. 81.
24 See also below Part III Chapter 1.1.
25 Hayek, Friedrich A. v.: *Law, Legislation and Liberty*. Volume I. Chicago and London 1973, p. 14; Volume III. Chicago and London 197, p. 70.
26 Hayek, *Komplexe Phänomene*, p. 15 ff.
27 Malik, *Management*, p. 32. (Translation by C. Malik)
28 Beer, Stafford: *Decision and Control*. Chichester 1994, p. 255.
29 Beer, *Heart*, p. 32.
30 Compare also Beer, *Heart*, p. 36 ff.
31 Compare for this, Ashby and Beer, *Heart*.
32 Ashby, p. 207.
33 Beer, *Heart*, p. 89.
34 Beer, *Heart*, p. 4.
35 Beer, Stafford: *Brain of the Firm*. Chichester 1994, p. 75.
36 Beer, *Heart*, p. 113ff; compare also Malik, Fredmund: *Strategie des Managements Komplexer Systeme*. 8th Edition. Bern, Stuttgart and Wien 2003, p. 112.
37 Beer, *Heart*, p. 262.
38 Beer, *Brain*, p. 155.
39 Beer, *Heart*, p. 93ff, p. 113ff; Beer, *Brain*, p. 119ff, p. 157ff; Malik, *Strategie*, p. 115ff, p. 492 ff.
40 Beer, *Heart*, p. 95.
41 Beer, *Heart*, p. 173ff; Beer, *Brain*, p. 124ff p. 167ff; Malik, p. 128ff, p. 499.
42 Beer, *Heart*, p. 199ff; Beer, *Brain*, p. 157ff; Malik, *Strategie*, p. 131ff, 501 ff.
43 See also below »The Principle of Autonomy«.
44 Beer, *Heart*, p. 225; Beer, *Brain*, p. 181; Malik, *Strategie*, p. 140ff, p. 506.
45 Beer, *Heart*, p. 251ff; Beer, *Brain*, p. 201; Malik, *Strategie*, p. 149ff, 507 ff.
46 Beer, *Heart*, p. 250.
47 Beer, *Heart*, p. 94.
48 Beer, *Heart*, p. 127 f.

49 Malik, *Strategie*, p. 101.
50 Beer, *Heart*, p. 116.
51 Beer, *Brain*, p. 155.
52 Beer, *Brain*, p. 228.
53 Beer, according to Malik, *Strategie*, p. 103.
54 For a detailed discussion of the reasons see Beer, *Heart*, p. 307 ff.
55 Malik, *Strategie*, p. 99.
56 Malik, *Strategie*, p. 102.
57 Beer, according to Malik, *Strategie*, p. 106.
58 Malik, *Strategie*, p. 103 ff.
59 Malik, *Strategie*, p. 105.
60 Beer, *Heart*, p. 113ff; compare also Malik, *Strategie*, p. 112.
61 Malik, *Strategie*, p. 112.
62 Malik, *Strategie*, p. 113.
63 Malik, *Strategie*, p. 113.
64 Beer, *Heart*, p. 92 f.
65 Hayek, *Liberty*, Vol. I, p. 8 ff.; Vol. III, p. xii; Tarnas, Richard: *Idee und Leidenschaft: Die Wege des westlichen Denkens*. München 1997, p. 347 ff.
66 Hayek, *Liberty*, Vol. I, p. 9 f.
67 Hayek, *Liberty*, Vol. I, p. 9 f.
68 Hayek, *Liberty*, Vol. I, p. 35 ff.
69 Ferguson according to Hayek, *Liberty*, Vol. I, p. 20.
70 Hayek, *Liberty*, Vol. I, p. 14.
71 Hayek, *Liberty*, Vol. I, p. 17.
72 See above Part II »Complex systems and variety«
73 Hayek, *Liberty*, Vol. I, p. 14; Vol. III, p. 70
74 Prechter, *Wave Principle*, p. 147ff; Hayek, *Liberty*, Vol. III, p. 160.
75 Riesman, David: *The Lonely Crowd*. Yale 1961, p. 19ff; Pelzmann, Linda. *Wirtschaftspsychologie*. 3rd Edition. Wien 2000, p. XXX.
76 Kirchgässner, Gebhard: *Homo Oeconomicus*. 2nd Edition. Tübingen 2000, p. 12.
77 Pelzmann, Linda: *M.o.M. Malik on Management*. November 2002, p. 186f; Kirchgässner, p. 2.
78 Arthur, W. Brian: »Inductive Reasoning and Bounded Rationality (The El Farol Problem)«, in: *American Economic Review (Papers and Proceedings)*. Vol. 84, 406, 1994.
79 Tversky, Amos/Kahneman, Daniel: »Rational Choice and the Framing of Decisions«, in: Kahneman, Daniel/Tversky, Amos (Eds.): *Choices, Values, and Frames*. Cambridge 2000., p. 221.
80 Sunstein, Cass R.: *Behavioral Law and Economics*. Cambridge 2000, p. 14.
81 Daniel Kahneman was awarded the Nobel Price »for having integrated insights from psychological research into economic science, especially concerning human judgment and decision-making under uncertainty», nobelprize.org.
82 Beer, *Heart*, p. 119; Malik, *Strategie*, p. 557.
83 Riesman, p. 21.

84 Pelzmann, Linda/Malik, Constantin/Miklautz, Michaela: »The critical mass of preferences for customization«, in: Blecker, Thorsten/Friedrich, Gerhard (Eds.): *Mass Customization: Concepts, Tools, Realization.* Berlin 2005, p. 328; Pelzmann, *M.o.M.*, p. 193.

85 Drucker, Peter: *The Frontiers of Management: Where Tomorrow's Decisions are Being Shaped Today.* New York 1986, p. 348f; note: Drucker's term *mass* is synonymous with the term *crowd* used here.

86 Le Bon, Gustave: *Psychologie des foules.* 7th Edition. Paris 2002, p. 10.

87 See for example Reich, Wilhelm: *Die Massenpsychologie des Faschismus.* Köln 1970

88 Le Bon, Paris 2002, p. 4.

89 Le Bon, Paris 2002, p. 15.

90 Le Bon, Gustave: *The Crowd: A Study of the Popular Mind.* 1896. Kitchener, Ont. 2001, p. 4; compare also McDougall, p. 31.

91 Drucker, *Frontiers*, p. 346f; again, Drucker's *mass* is synonymous with *crowd.*

92 Le Bon, Paris 2002, p. 9.

93 Le Bon, Paris 2002, p. 9 f.

94 Le Bon, Kitchener 2001, p 14.

95 Le Bon, Paris 2002, p. 93 ff.

96 Freud, Sigmund : *Massenpsychologie und Ich-Analyse.* 6th Edition. Frankfurt 2002, p. 56; Most of Freud's accurate observations are based on Le Bon. Unfortunately, he then falls back into psychoanalysis.

97 McDougall, William: *The Group Mind.* New York 1920, p. 31 f.

98 Canetti, Elias: *Crowds and Power.* New York 1973, p. 53 f.

99 Pelzmann *M.o.M.*, p. 193 and 194.

100 Pelzmann et al., p. 329.

101 Pelzmann *M.o.M.*, p. 190.

102 Canetti, p. 16.

103 See below 2. Socionomics – the science of social prediction.

104 Canetti, p. 43 ff.

105 Le Bon, Paris 2002, p 9 ff.

106 Canetti, p. 30 ff.

107 Canetti, p. 30.

108 Le Bon, Paris 2002, p. 17 ff.

109 Festinger, Leon: »Informal Social Communication«, in: *Psychological Review*, Vol 57 1950, p. 271–282.

110 Le Bon, Paris 2002, S. 13.

111 Prechter, *Wave Principle*, p. 164 ff.

112 See Gladwell, *The Tipping Point*; Prechter, *Wave Principle*, p. 164 ff.

113 *The Economist*, May 14th 2005, p. 77 f.

114 Canetti, p. 30 f.

115 Canetti, p. 43 ff.

116 Le Bon. Paris 2002, p. 60, 85 ff.

117 Le Bon, Paris 2002, p. 17; Freud, p. 40; Ortega y Gasset, José: *Der Aufstand der Massen.* Stuttgart and München 2002, p. 101.
118 Freud, p. 45.
119 Prechter, *Wave Principle*, p. 150 ff.
120 Hayek, *Liberty*, Vol. I, p. 75.
121 Hayek, *Liberty*, Vol. I, p. 74.
122 Prechter, *Wave Principle*, p. 157.
123 Pelzmann, *M.o.M*, p. 195.
124 Le Bon, Paris 2002, p. 5.
125 Frost, Alfred J./Prechter, Robert, R.: *Elliott Wave Principle.* Gainsville 1998, p. 19; Prechter, *Wave Principle*, p. 23.
126 Frost/Prechter, p. 19.
127 Frost/Prechter, p. 21; Prechter, *Wave Principle*, p. 24.
128 I prefer to use the expression *level of recursion* as it is common in cybernetics. The expression used by Elliott and Prechter is *degree.* Although simpler, the word degree is used for many things and I, therefore, find that *level of recursion* expresses more clearly what is meant. Moreover, if we have a coherent terminology it is clearer and easier to see where the common features of both cybernetics and Socionomics lie.
129 Prechter, *Wave Principle*, p. 26.
130 Prechter, *Wave Principle*, p. 26 f.
131 Prechter, *Wave Principle*, p. 28.
132 Prechter, *Wave Principle*, p. 28.
133 Prechter, *Wave Principle*, p. 56 f.
134 Prechter, *Wave Principle*, p. 56 f.
135 Prechter, *Wave Principle*, p. 56.
136 www.goldennumber.net.
137 Prechter, *Wave Principle*, p. 61.
138 Elliot, Ralph N.: *Nature's Law.* 1946, p. 65.
139 Siegfried, according to Prechter, *Wave Principle*, p. 186.
140 Prechter, *Wave Principle*, p. 69.
141 Prechter, *Wave Principle*, p. 170 ff.
142 Prechter, *Wave Principle*, p. 76.
143 Prechter, *Wave Principle*, p. 75.
144 Prechter, *Wave Principle*, p. 50.
145 Prechter, *Wave Principle*, p. 75.
146 Prechter, *Wave Principle*, p. 75.
147 Prechter, *Wave Principle*, p. 66 f.
148 Prechter, *Wave Principle*, p. 194 f.
149 Prechter, *Wave Principle*, p. 191.
150 Prechter, *Wave Principle*, p. 196.
151 Prechter, *Wave Principle*, p. 198.
152 Prechter, *Wave Principle*, p. 187.
153 Prechter, *Wave Principle*, p. 50.

154 Prechter, *Wave Principle*, 145 ff.
155 Prechter, *Wave Principle*, p. 147 f.
156 Prechter, *Wave Principle*, p. 148.
157 Prechter, *Wave Principle*, p. 149.
158 MacLean according to Prechter, *Wave Principle*, p. 149.
159 Prechter, *Wave Principle*, p. 150.
160 Prechter, *Wave Principle*, p. 151.
161 Prechter, *Wave Principle*, p. 151.
162 Prechter, *Wave Principle*, p. 163.
163 Prechter, *Wave Principle*, p. 150.
164 Prechter, *Wave Principle*, p. 157.
165 Hayek, *Liberty*, Vol. I, p. 75.
166 Prechter, *Wave Principle*, p. 152.
167 Pigou according to Shiller: *The New York Times*, February 4, 2001.
168 Prechter, *Wave Principle*, p. 153.
169 Prechter, *Wave Principle*, p. 155.
170 Prechter, *Wave Principle*, p. 158.
171 Bonabeau, Eric/Meyer, Christopher: »Swarm Intelligence: A Whole New Way to Think About Business«, in: *Harvard Business Review* May 2001.
172 Hayek, *Liberty*, Vol. I, p. 18.
173 Hayek, *Liberty*, Vol. III, p. 159.
174 Prechter, *Wave Principle*, p. 203.
175 Prechter, *Wave Principle*, p. 203 ff.
176 Lefevre according to Prechter, *Wave Principle*, p. 204.
177 Prechter, *Wave Principle*, p. 206.
178 Prechter, *Wave Principle*, p. 227.
179 Prechter, *Wave Principle*, p. 6.
180 Prechter, *Wave Principle*, p. 227.
181 Prechter, *Wave Principle*, p. 228.
182 Prechter, *Wave Principle*, p. 229.
183 Prechter, *Wave Principle*, p. 235.
184 Prechter, *Wave Principle*, p. 235.
185 Prechter, *Wave Principle*, p. 260.
186 Prechter, *Wave Principle*, p. 255.
187 Prechter, *Wave Principle*, p. 329 f.
188 *The Elliott Wave Theorist*. September 2004.
189 Prechter, *Wave Principle*, p. 234; *degrees of trend* would in our vocabulary translate into *levels of recursion of trend*.
190 Hayek, *Komplexe Phänomene*.
191 Popper, Karl: *Eine Welt der Propensitäten*. Tübingen 1995.
192 Beer, *Heart*, p. 338 f.
193 Prechter, *Wave Principle*, p. 402.
194 Prechter, *Wave Principle*, p. 404.
195 Prechter, *Wave Principle*, p. 407.

196 Dewey, Edward R./Dakin, Edwin F.: *Cycles: The Science of Prediction.* 5th Ed. New York 1947, p. 51ff.
197 Schumpeter, Joseph A. *Essays*, 6th Ed. New Brunswick 2003, p. 22; Mager, Nathan H. *The Kondratieff Waves.* New York 1987, p. 17.
198 Gerster, p. 7.
199 Mager, p. 17f; Solomou, Solomos: *Phases of Economic Growth, 1850 – 1973: Kondratieff Waves and Kuznets Swings.* 2nd Ed. Cambridge 1989, p. 83.
200 Mager, p. 18; Solomou, p. 10ff.
201 Mager, p. 24ff. For a detailed discussion of the different stages see Malik, *M.o.M.*, p. 12ff.
202 Schumpeter, J. A.: *Business Cycles.* New York and London, 1939.
203 Thomas, p. 11.
204 Perez, Carlota: »*Neue Technologien und sozio-institutioneller Wandel*«, in: Thomas, H./Nefiodow, L. A.: *Kondratieffs Zyklen der Wirtschaft: An der Schwelle neuer Vollbeschaeftigung?* Herford 1998, p. 18.
205 Thomas, Hans: »*Zur Einführung*«, in: Thomas, H./Nefiodow, L. A.: *Kondratieffs Zyklen der Wirtschaft: An der Schwelle neuer Vollbeschaeftigung?* Herford 1998, p. 13.
206 See for example Gottfried Bombach: *Lange Wellen*, or Solomos Solomou, *Phases of Economic Growth.*
207 Malik, *M.o.M.*, p. 16.
208 Bühl, Walter L.: *Sozialer Wandel im Ungleichgewicht.* Stuttgart 1990, p. 59.
209 Eddington, according to Dewey/Dawkin, p. 195.
210 Perez, *Thought Leader*, p. 7.
211 Popper, p. 37.
212 Popper, p. 28ff.
213 Popper, p. 36ff.
214 Leonard, Alenna: *Between momentum and control: a dynamic of democracy*, 2005. (Unpublished paper)
215 For this see Livas, J.: *The Cybernetic State.* Mexico City 2003.
216 Beer, *Heart*, p. 233f.
217 Ziembinski, p. 43ff; Morison, p. 5ff.
218 Müller, p. 6f.
219 See Hayek, *Liberty*, Vol. III, p. 13ff., 143ff.
220 This in itself is already a »crowd problem« as Peter Drucker in his book *The New Realities* brilliantly observes (London 1989, p. 93ff.).
221 Hayek, *Liberty*, Vol. III, p. 3ff.
222 Hayek, *Liberty*, Vol. III, p. 16.
223 Hayek, *Liberty*, Vol. III, p. 15.
224 Hayek, *Liberty*, Vol. III, p. 103.
225 Hayek, *Liberty*, Vol. III, p. 37.
226 *Constitution of the United States*, Article 1 Section 3.
227 Hayek, *Law, Legislation and Liberty*, 1973–1979.
228 Hayek, *Liberty*, Vol. I, p. 1.

229 For Hayeks understanding of Law see Vol. I, Chapters 4–6.
230 Hayek, *Liberty*, Vol. III, p. 109.
231 Beer, *Heart*, p. 251 ff.
232 This chapter is based largely on *The Elliott Wave Theorist.* September 2004.
233 *The Elliott Wave Theorist.* September 2004, p. 5.
234 *The Elliott Wave Theorist.* September 2004.
235 Beer, *Heart*, p. 235f, 242f; Beer, *Brain*, p. 268 ff.
236 Hetzler, Sebastian: »Die Architektur richtiger Entscheidungen«, in: *Online Blatt,* Malik Management Zentrum St. Gallen, August 2005, p. 3–6. The following description of the Operations Room is based on this article.
237 Hetzler, p. 6.
238 It is clear that these are specific values of modern western societies. In other societies there might be other values that are fundamental to the identity of society. Here, clearly, no general list can be given but each case is to be looked at separately and independently.
239 Note: In Switzerland no such majority is needed because of the direct democratic factor.
240 *Constitution of the United States*, Article 5.
241 *Grundgesetz für die Bundesrepublik Deutschland*, Artikel 79 Absatz 2.
242 For a general overview of legislative instruments see Böckel, Markus. *Instrumente der Einpassung neuen Rechts in die Rechtsordnung.* Berlin 1993; Müller, *Elemente einer Rechtssetzungslehre.*
243 Böckel, p. 53 f.
244 Prechter, *Wave Principle*, p. 403.
245 Gauch, Peter/Schluep, Walter R./Schmid, Jörg/Rey, Heinz: *Schweizerisches Obligationenrecht Allgemeiner Teil.* Vol. II, 8th Edition, Zürich 2003, p. 364.
246 See below »Possible jurisprudential obstacles to anticipatory legislation«
247 Müller, p. 41.
248 Müller, p. 41.
249 Böckel, p. 42 ff.
250 Häfelin, Ulrich/Haller, Walter: *Schweizerisches Bundesstaatsrecht.* 6th Edition. Zürich 2005, p. 528 f.
251 Häfelin, Ulrich/Müller, Georg: *Allgemeines Verwaltungsrecht.* 4th Edition. Zürich 2002, p. 130.
252 Rehbinder, Manfred: *Einführung in die Rechtswissenschaft.* 8th Edition. Berlin 1995, p. 151 f.
253 See below 6.2. Prohibition of arbitrary decision-making.
254 See for example *Bundesverfassung der Schweizerischen Eidgenossenschaft*, Artikel 9.
255 Häfelin/Müller, p. 111; Häfelin/Haller, p. 234.
256 Janis, Irving Lester: *Groupthink: psychological studies of policy decisions and fiascoes.* 2nd Edition. Boston 1982.
257 Festinger, *Informal Social Communication.*

258 Festinger, Leon/Thibaut, John: »Interpersonal Communication in small groups«, in: *Journal of abnormal social Psychology*, Vol. 46 1951, p. 92–99
259 Le Bon, Kitchener 2001, p. 115.
260 Le Bon, Kitchener 2001, p. 115.
261 Beer, *Heart*, p. 375f; 499ff.
262 Max Planck according to Prechter, *Wave Principle*, p. 13.

Index